MW01520031

Author: Christine Brandon

Copyright © 1999, 2001, 2020

I dedicate this book to my children who convinced me that my story needed to be shared.

Many thanks for their patience and support.

Author's Note

Diana hopes that this book can be a healing experience, and a voice for many that could never speak of their most hurtful secrets. It was intended to set many people free from barriers and burdens of a heritage that holds them hostage. As they honor their heritage, may they be free to follow their own stars. Diana's humble life was a testament of the unlimited power and strength everyone holds within his own soul to overcome adversity and challenges – against all odds.

This is a non-fiction book with true events. Some names were changed to protect the few innocent. It was written for those who desire to grow, to overcome, and wish to be free. It has not been sugar-coated for those that are faint at heart.

Who would benefit from reading this book?

Anyone who may struggle with life issues like;

Trying to break the chains of the expectation of others Authoritarian upbringing

Examining his/her loyalties and false heroes

Dealing with unfair, unjust, discriminatory situations
Relationship to religions

A cult

Unexpected and /or unwanted sexual advances or assault
Sheltered childhood/betrayed innocence

Bad marriage or unhealthy alliances
Childhood trauma

War memories.

Control, oppression of free feelings.

Table of Contents

Reader's comments:

"I was immediately drawn into the story. I had a very vivid and real feeling of the events and circumstances, a strong visual and emotional impression. I felt what the author felt. I wanted to be her friend. I was there." LouAnn D.

"This book makes you examine your heritage. I was dramatically moved by the courage of its content." Barry M.

"My husband and I cried throughout a couple of chapters. Some of the issues were ours. We've been there." Donette B.

"I couldn't put it down" Karin H.

"I challenge anyone to read the first three chapters without shedding a tear" Steven M.

"I am deeply affected by the story. My family can't stop talking about it. I am hoping to find the courage to change some things in my life." C.S.

Prelude

Her life was safe. No one really knew her. It was better that way. She was the heroine that left, the one that broke out of the norm and had a perfect life ever after. No one knew that behind the facades of roses and ivies, behind pristine fences around the "Good" and the "Holy" there were brittle walls and burning skies and scars of the war. No one was there when the structures she counted on crumbled, nor when the heroes she trusted betrayed her innocence and chained her soul. No one knew.

Diana wondered today if she could ever break free of those chains. She was held hostage by her heritage.

She wondered today why she buried the story she wrote, the finished autobiography, in her drawer for the last twenty years. Why? What was she still hiding from? Was she trying to be kind to others or herself by hiding behind those pages, so careful not to throw stones, tell too much, not to offend or expose anyone? Today she decided to open herself to her own vulnerability as well as to the judgement of others, and let all the ripples of her life run their course. She would let the times speak for themselves in all their nakedness and simplicity.

I

CHILD   OF   TIMES

Diana's life was fine. She was at peace with the world and with herself… secure, content, happy and healthy…she thought. She had a loving husband, a most beautiful home, and wonderful children and grandchildren. She enjoyed lavishing on them everything she did not have and everything she had now. Diana certainly felt blessed with more than she could have ever wished for and could have ever imagined.

The abundance of this good life sometimes scared her, but most of the time she was successful in quieting down those faint ripples in her deepest conscious mind. But then and there was a nightmare again.

If she counted her blessings every day, would it stay this way, would it be less likely for this life of hers to crash, or in an instant be taken away?

For now Diana treasured this "calm," a first in her life. She could hide and heal in this peaceful environment. Had it not been for her 11-year-old precious granddaughter, nothing would have changed.

She had a school project, Elise said, and she needed to know how different her grandmother's childhood was from hers.

Not her childhood! Diana's heart sank. Never in her life did she talk about that subject. There were a few years of her childhood that she would rather not remember because they left a mark on her life that she would never be able to erase. In her nightmares she still felt the trucks rolling by, shaking the ground, soldiers marching to their beat, boots stomping the snow. She still hated every red sky.

To open that door to the war-ridden years of her childhood would turn her world upside down. Really, would it take a child to do that? The next morning Diana woke up to a red sky. Good Lord, a red sky! Morgenrot! Before she realized she found herself humming "Morgenrot, Morgenrot". She had hummed that song many times. She would have liked to think that it was just a catchy tune lingering in her memory. Why did it still leave her with a chill, an uneasy feeling, as if it was a bad omen for the day? Her sister used to sing that song. It was one of many war songs Diana learned as a child. They always haunted her. This one still ruins her day. "Morgenrot, Morgenrot, leuchtest mir zum fruehen Tod. Bald wird die Trompete blasen, dann muss ich mein Leben lassen, ich und mancher Kamerad."It translates: "Red morning sky, red morning sky, the sign of my impending death. Soon I'll hear the trumpets glare, and I will have to give my life, along with many of my friends." The read skies, she remembered, were the bombs raining down on the cities on the other side of their mountains.

When did that war stop? Did it stop? Time seemed only a thin veil stretched over more than a half a century. The beat of the war drums was still echoing in Diana's ears. Why would she talk about these things now – so many years later, when she finally stood on high grounds, secure, safe enough to think that her life couldn't shatter around her any more. Or could it? She was never sure.

To open that door would be a painful venture, she knew, like brushing up on an old would and feeling the hurt again as if it were new and fresh and had only just happened

Elise was determined.

Diana finally figured that she could just talk about the *good things*, the *ordinary*, *normal* things of her childhood. Whatever that was. She decided that the child was no threat, she wouldn't ask for much.

Elise kept asking. As if Diana was watching from afar, she felt her inquisitive granddaughter tiptoeing over her past - innocently enough.

"*Of course things were different*", Diana said. *I grew up during the time of The Depression and WWII, in a small Bavarian village I thought of as the end of the world. My parents were very poor. My father built our small house, and my mother made everything in it. The cupboards were empty most of the time, the bread drawer locked and the house was cold. We went to sleep with the birds, hoping to wake up in the morning, by the grace of God.*

In my childhood home there were no electric appliances. Imagine yourself without television, refrigerators, washers and dryers, microwaves, dishwashers, computers or calculators, fax machines or copy machines. We did not have a radio or a telephone.

People were very resourceful and self-sufficient though; they knew how to make almost everything necessary to survive. They built their houses, made their furniture and all their clothes, all the tools of the trades and utensils of all kinds. They hunted the wild animals, butchered cows, sheep, goats, chickens for food, and learned how to preserve meats, eggs, berries, potatoes and many other foods for the winter without freezers. There were no stores or factories, and most people had no money to buy things anyway.

We didn't know ice cream or coke, pizza, corn, peanut butter or McDonald's. There were no toasters or coffeemakers or hairdryers, Velcro or gym shoes, not even hot water. Most people had no running water in the house, and had to pump all their water from a well. The laundry was scrubbed outside by the well on a washboard, boiled on the stove if necessary and dried outside. In the cold weather the clothes froze on the line outside; stiff and rigid they looked like pinned-up petrified ghosts. The iron was just that: a block of iron that was heated on top of the wood-burning stove. We had to heat up water to bathe, and our only tub was a wood bucket. There were no showers.

There were no baby diapers or any fancy baby things. The babies scooted around on the floor, and if they dirtied themselves they were taken outside to the animal's water trough by the well in summer or winter and cleaned up with cold water splashed on their bottoms. This may be the reason why we were potty-trained very early, the latest by six or seven months. I credit it to the brave babies rather than to the proud and efficient mothers.

We had to feed and milk our cow, named Scheckei (Spotty), and clean up manure. I mean "we," because as children we were very much involved in all the chores of the household. "Was Haenschen nicht lernt, lernt Hans nimmermehr", my mother would say. It means, "What little Johnny doesn't learn, big John never will." I remember we would recite our multiplication tables during chores often, as our entire schoolwork had to be in our head, without the help of any textbooks and electronic gadgets. We used to churn butter from fresh, unpasteurized milk. I remember it, because it took an eternity of churning before the little butter flakes developed, and finally clumped together in a ball. It was the best butter.

Most American homes at that time had electricity and many modern conveniences unheard of in our little village in Germany. We had no electricity in our entire house. There was an oil lamp, and if we were out of oil, a candle in the kitchen, and you had to feel your way around the rest of the house in the dark. There were no streetlights either.

The toilets were outhouses. Ours was modern. It was upstairs, inside. Our father enclosed a small space on the side of our house. There was a board with a hole, and when you sat on it and went, you could hear it fall down the 2 stories into the hole in the ground, and the wind would blow up from below and literally "freeze your bottom off".

There were no gas stoves or barbecues. The only heat source for the entire house was the wood-burning oven in the kitchen. Some people could even afford coals. We were lucky to have enough wood for the long winters. No one, of course, had a car in our family, or in most families. There were some motorcycles in town, and old bicycles with huge tires. My family didn't have either. We walked. Cars and motorcycles couldn't have climbed the steep hills anyway, even if there had been roads. On the one road into town a bus came most days in the morning and it went back to the city 60 miles away in the evening. That bus left a sickening trail of Diesel exhaust that I still smell.

There was one Food-and General Store in town, and the women walked the three or four miles every day, that is, if they had money. This was a social event. There wasn't much for women to do in town for recreation. You'd never see any of them dressed casually, in work-clothes, with rollers in their hair, etc. They wore the only set of good clothes they had. They had a reputation to keep. It wasn't just picking up the daily needs from the butcher, the baker... it was also a chance to stay abreast of the most current events and latest gossip. No one ever had to worry about getting enough exercise. This daily shopping trip is still customary in many German towns today.

We had a very smart cat named Peter, and a white kitten named Mitzi, that kept running away. A blind lady in the village found her one day and took her in. I had to give my kitten to that blind lady then, because she could see a hint of white when she looked at this cat, the only thing she had ever seen in her life. I learned charity early. Peter took care of Pest Control, we never saw a mouse around.

I remember my first day of school – only because the teacher took away my little lunch bag, storing it high up on the windowsill near the ceiling of the classroom. That's the only thing I could think about the entire morning. This lunch bag was my security; without it I would most certainly go hungry. I knew what hunger was. Every child was given a "School-Tuete", a big cone bag, to celebrate the first day of school. It contained pencils, an apple, a couple of candies, some chalk, and a small sulfur chalkboard to write on, because paper was in short supply. If the teacher became angry with a child he would break this chalkboard over the child's head. It happened to most kids at one time or another. My brother came home with one broken chalkboard too many. My father wouldn't buy him another one. When the teacher asked him why he was writing on one of the broken pieces, he said that his father wanted the teacher to buy him a new one. My brother remembers it as a very disrespectful and defiant thing to say to his teacher. He was afraid of some consequence. However the teacher didn't want to deal with my father, I guess. The next day he gave him a new chalkboard.

Three quarters of the year was winter in our part of the country. We had so much snow that often our house and many others were buried up to the roof, and we had to climb out of our attic window or dig out our door from the inside. Some roofs would touch the ground, which was the invitation for us as children to ski up to, the peak. It was the perfect ski run. One house that was particularly suitable belonged to a 100 year-old lady who used to chase us with her cane. We thought of her as a witch anyway for "obvious" reasons: her entire house was plastered with holy pictures and strange artifacts. She could hear her ceiling rumble when we skied up on top of her roof. We never were caught, or we would have been in serious trouble.

The snow plough often couldn't get through, when 4-5 feet of snow accumulated over night. Then there was one person per household designated to shovel out the miles of road. These crews would work all day shoveling. They had to throw the snow over the often 12 foot high bank on the side of the road.

Not everyone had shoes. We were lucky that our father knew how to make wooden shoes. The only shoes we owned were wooden clogs. Our "house-slippers" were braided strips of straw or old clothing. Our skies were also homemade. We would tie them to our shoes with leather strips. In the winter we could only leave the house on skis; we'd get lost in the snow otherwise. That is how we learned to ski at age 3 or so. We had nearly frozen heels and toes many times. To dare the elements of nature was every child's fun then, as it is now. The kids down the street would go sledding in their underwear and bare feet. It was not unusual for people to walk barefoot in the snow. Occasionally the people who had huge sleds to pull lumber and supplies with would pull children as well. To catch a ride on a sled like that was a big treat; it felt like a ride in a convertible today.

We had no roller skates, or ice skates, though I do remember nailing a piece of tin from an old tin can to the bottom of my wooden shoes. Some boys had figured out that you could really fly on the ice. Besides, the wooden shoes were often very cumbersome, as the snow would stick to them and "ball up", making it hard to walk. This "tin"-idea was the solution for this problem and it also made the shoes better than ice skates - and almost worth the trouble I got in – when the nails split the wood of my shoes. My father must have understood the fun I had though, because he made me another pair of wooden shoes the next day. Perhaps he thought these skates were not such a bad idea.

I wouldn't miss a day of school, even in the worst of winter. It was the only way to get out of the house. I had to walk or ski 3 miles to school, and I would cry until my mother let me go despite the worst snowstorms. Just a few kids would show up, and the teachers acted as if they were so proud of us for coming. We would warm up by the big oven, and sometimes even had a hot lunch. It really was much more fun than staying home where there was nothing to do besides chores. There was always the rule: "Erst die Arbeit, dann das Spiel", meaning first the work, then the playtime. My mother always found more chores for us to do, and there was a law at our house that no one sat down unless everything was done.

The summers were short, and on the rare occasions we didn't have to work in the fields with our parents, we had fun with simple things. We amused ourselves with herds of pinecone cows in a pretend stable in the woods, catching butterflies and June bugs, or bake potatoes in a fire. Sometimes the neighbor's boys let me help watching a heard of cows. It was their job, and not an easy one, to keep them within the boundaries of the farmer's meadows. We swore these cows had brains. They either liked you or not. If not, they could be quite willful and nasty. My

14

brother told me once, never to underestimate a cow. He had a job tending a farmer's cows at age 12 or so. He and some of his friends would tease this one particular cow that did not like "skirts." They dared my brother to steal one of his sister/s skirts, and this cow chased him across several fields, finally into a ditch, at which point he stumbled and was mauled by the cow until he rolled up in a ball and played dead. The cow then stood herself over him, and urinated on him.

Those were fun times out in the fields. I was ecstatic when the boys let me hang out with them. That was rarely. I would not go home hungry, because we made a fire and baked potatoes that we stole right out of the ground. We would pick mushrooms and berries, or collect grasses, roots and weeds such as caraway seed and herbs for our mother. Many hours we would sit in a cherry tree stealing a neighbor's cherries, eating our fill... Sitting in a cherry tree, removed from the rest of the world, hugged and protected by the leaves all around – it was a highlight in my life. I cherish the thought today.

I remember when a few of us girls would pin a T-shirt together at the crotch for a "swimsuit" we had seen a picture of, and we would go "swimming", that is flailing around in a nearby brook in a few inches of water. There were no swimming pools or rivers near us, but this was all I could handle anyway. I was trying very hard to overcome my secret apprehension of water. I was deathly afraid of drowning. I never learned to swim, and the thought of a lot of water was always very overwhelming for me. Besides this "swimming" was one of the secrets that our parents could never find out. A swimsuit was "indecent"; no one had one. You were always supposed to be fully clothed, especially in someone's company.

My sister got in trouble once when she went "swimming" with her three girlfriends. They hung their panties on a fence, and when they came out of the water, all the pantys were gone. Their brothers had spied on them, stolen their panties and taken them home to their mothers. My sister wore her one and only pink "Sunday"- panties. There was no mistake that they were hers, and mother knew before she returned home. My sister was given a lesson on decency and such things.

There were no movie theaters or swimming pools, libraries or park district activities, camp, girl scouts, etc. where we lived. I was always alone. The few kids that lived anywhere near us I often wasn't allowed to play with for reasons I didn't understand at the time. I always had to come straight home after school. We lived between two villages, both three to four miles away. How I wished I could have hung out with the popular kids in town! I wanted to be one of them. I always felt like I didn't belong.

My parents were very selective about who my friends were. I didn't understand yet the turmoil and disappointments and dissolution of grownups with regards to relationships, friendships and relatives. My father said that you don't really know a person until you have "eaten a sack of salt" with him.

Today I know that you only need one good friend in life.

As a child however I wanted to be friends with everyone, I wanted to trust everyone. I desperately needed people around me. I felt like an only child since my brothers and sisters were so much older and away from home most of the time. We were so isolated. I often faulted my parents for not allowing me more friends and social contacts - whatever few were even possible. I remember how ecstatic I would be when someone would visit.

I suppose my parents were worried about me. My mother had an awesome gut instinct about people. She could smell a rat a mile away, and would not trust someone easily. She would look someone in the eyes, and instantly make up her mind about him.

Today I wish I had trusted my instincts more often.

There was a plaque my mother made that hung above our front door, and instead of "Welcome" it said in so many words: Tell me who your friends are, and I'll tell you who you are. It was considered a lesser evil to be alone and lonesome than keeping the wrong company.

Would you say that my parents were snobs? Were they simply overprotective of us? We were deprived of much. Was this the worst of evils? We learned lessons for a lifetime. We didn't have gangs and graffiti, or drugs, or guns… so… did we really miss so much?

"The times of my childhood were very different than yours", she told Elise. "It was a primitive way of life, cruel and unfair and cold, but the lessons taught us to survive. They were war times. We had no choices like you do today. We were not free. How lucky you are to live in this great country! You can be whatever you want to be."

Diana's granddaughter was impressed. It was more than enough for her to handle. She got an "A" on her paper. She herself thought it was a job well done. Actually it was surprisingly painless. So far.

However, Diana's daughter kept prodding. She wanted more. She said, "Elise learned more about your life than I ever could."

This was true. There was another life, another time that Diana had deleted as though it never happened. There was another her that no one knew. It took her years to bury the secrets at the bottom of the sea. She kept them safe. She never shared them with her children while they were growing up. It wasn't too long ago that everything settled, and the nightmares stopped at last. Why disturb the muddy waters? Why take a chance now to get caught up in a riptide or current that would cause unrest, or bring things to the surface?

Was it the right time to open the door to her past, now that she may be able to look back with some resolve and forgiveness and not too much pain?

Diana's daughter's frustration disturbed her. After all, there are legitimate secrets to have, she defended, but there was value to examining the past because her legacy was her children's legacy as well. She asked herself as she was looking at her life as a whole: Are we products of our environment, of our ancestry, of wars or crimes? Are we victims of fate? Can we influence our predetermined destiny? Can we "override" the program written – that fate has cursed us with, or that God has given us?

Do we have choices? If so, are those choices the free intentions of our own soul? Freedom was not her birthright. Freedom – the right to live, think, speak, choose without constraint from within or without – is a divine gift, a luxury not everyone enjoys, even while living in this "land of the free".

Are we forever held prisoners within our own souls by the chains of the past, the shadows of history and heritage, culture, legacy and loyalty Diana asked herself? Are we forever held hostage by the chains of betrayal, intimidation and fear, blame and guilt?

Can anyone break these chains? Will the tremors of her past ever fade?

Diana believed it was possible – in the best of times, for the strong and the free. In the worst of times, however, it would take so much more... a strong will to overcome, a passionate desire to succeed, the freedom to make choices, and more than a little faith. They say that the power is within us. It determines the course and it can set us free.

Someday, Diana hoped to clearly see the reflections of herself in the mighty river of time.

"I am writing," Diana decided... "I will do so – not in polished and exquisite terms. I will not dress them up or down, but I'll let the times speak for themselves."

They were strange times, the times of her childhood.

II

NO   TEARS

Bavaria/Germany.

Records of Diana's hometown Waldeck date back to Roman times, some as far back as the 13th century. It became a village in 1704. At 1000 meters in altitude, it is the highest point of the Bavarian Forest. The land used to be owned by the Roman Catholic Church. Always was and is. The only significance of the town was that it was located on the "Salt Road". This "Golden Road" was documented as existing from 1000 AD and was a very important link as well as the only connection for trade, such as salt, between Passau, Bavaria and Prachatitz, Bohemia. Dead-ending at the border of Bohemia, now Czechoslovakia, in this remote corner of Bavaria, is Waldeck.

The land was totally barren and unlikely to be of use to farming or settling. It stood to reason because three quarters of the year was winter. However a bishop in the 14th century sent a few rugged settlers to this area to try cultivating the mountainous, rocky land, if at all possible.

Diana's father was born in 1896, and his family name dates back to Roman times, the year 260 AD. In the "Necktartal", the valley of the "Necktar"-river, a town was founded called by the same name. The records indicate that his family was descendent of a king. Historic documentation shows that the town not only survived the 30 year war from 1618-1648, but the plague in 1635, disasters of hurricanes, tornadoes, an earthquake in 1930, and numerous major floods. It was a very prosperous city then, and proof that these people were survivors. In the later years, research shows, Diana's ancestors moved to Bohemia and owned one of the oldest, famous glass-manufacturing companies.

At her time, they lived in a tiny village between Logan and Waldeck. The few houses and families in-between used the schoolhouse of one and the Post Office of the other town. It was strange to belong to neither town. Waldeck was nestled at the foot of the Lusen, a mountain of 1370 meters, with a population of approximately 800 people, including the few farmers that lived in the outlying areas. Their world ended at the ridge of the mountain. It was hard for everyone to survive. The few farmers were the fortunate ones; at least they had food to eat. It was a struggle for them to tend the rocky land and hope to harvest a crop in the short summers, to feed the small herds of pigs, cows, oxen and sheep. The rest of the people, including the hired hands of the farmers, and some self-taught tradesmen and entrepreneurs were poor. Outsiders considered their village as "van woid hint" (behind the forest), meaning "beyond civilization".

Diana was born in 1936. It was the time between World War I and World War II, when the entire world was in a depression. Life was more severe and desolate than ever in their little Bavarian town – an isolated pocket that time seemed to have forgotten. People still lived in the medieval ages, when humanity was considered irredeemably sinful and had value only through the infinite grace of God. Her parents were righteous people with integrity, goodness and honesty in their hearts. They were also poor. Poverty was only one of their virtues. They had strong ethics and excellent moral character, and their motto was "to do no harm". Life was hard. Work was a blessing. People were proud. Their wealth was in their honor. Women were inferior; their purpose was to bear and raise children and to obey and serve "the man". Children were seldom planned;

there was no birth control or abortion. The law was much in people's own hands. Survival was a challenge, and religion the only comfort.

In those times of war freedom was not a birthright. Theirs was a culture of no choice. Those were the times when Diana was born.

They were strange times. The rules were different. There were many rules for the children of their times, especially the children of the poor…"Honor thy mother and father" was a most sacred commandment. It was absolute law never to question authority. They were taught to subordinate themselves, and always obey and respect grownups; they were older and bigger, and therefore deserved their respect. They were not allowed to examine, question or judge. They had no right to speak, to want or to desire outside their lot in life. They had no right to their own feelings. They were born to be servants. As little children they learned the law of life: "cause and effect". There was discipline and honor and order.

There were no tears. By their parent's standards their children would never cry or show any emotions in public. They were never included in adult conversations, and to talk about other people's business was not allowed. "Etiquette" was important, and good manners were a must. Children were to be seen, not heard. They were taught to always be courteous, stand back and let someone else be first, to give their seat to the next, more deserving person. Modesty and humility were especially inbred in a girl. Their parents took great care to make sure they didn't get a big head. They were never to think that they were better than someone else was. Should they have done something exceptional, they were never to brag or show pride, because "Hochfahrt und Stolz" (arrogance and pride) were the worst evils. Diana's parents could not tell them that they were proud of them or show their approval – for fear it may make them arrogant. Diana could not accept a compliment gracefully her entire life. If she said "thank you" it was not without blushing and being embarrassed for drawing attention to herself. Arrogance was evil. Her mother always said, "Boasting about your talents or achievements only creates envy". Envy was another evil. There were many of those "capital sins".

Love was unspoken. With all the rules and commandments there was no room for much sentimentality. No one ever said: "I love you" or such things. Yet, they felt a strong bond even in the most adverse times, and they trusted that bond. There was an aura of caring in their family that extended somehow to all human kind and beyond. They had a respect for life – even though death and war surrounded them.

One of the earliest memories of Diana's childhood was this: She was about three years old. Her cousin came to visit with her little girl who was her age. The two played in front of her house with some gravel in the hole near the downspout, and Susie threw some in the street – just as a neighbor walked by. He came promptly up and asked which one of them was throwing the stones. He intended to discipline them, as would have been his right. He was an adult. Susie pointed to her. Diana was too surprised to speak. He turned her over his knee and spanked her. Her mother and her cousin came out and Diana hoped they had seen what had happened. Her little friend insisted she didn't throw the stones, and her mother believed her. Diana's mother would have never embarrassed a guest, so no one believed her. She envied Susie because her mother believed her. She felt betrayed that her mother would believe the word of a stranger over hers. The principles of her mother were hard to understand. She hated it. She remembered it well ever after. This was her first encounter with unfairness and injustice, and she wished she had learned to fight and speak up for herself. This was one of the times in Diana's life that she felt abandoned. The little girl knew the truth and she tried very hard to be her friend later, though she never could quite forgive her. She didn't know whom she felt more hurt by, her mother or her friend.

The traditions and customs were endless. A religious community – there were many "Holy Days" and pilgrimages, Krapfen and Eggs for Easter (a colored hardboiled egg in the center of a doughnut) which she remembered as the only gift they ever received from anyone outside of the family. A popular game in every family was knocking two eggs together – called "becken"; the egg that broke last, was the winner. It was a fun thing to do, but bittersweet, because there weren't many eggs to break. Besides, hers always broke first, and that meant she was out of the game.

People would take bread and eggs, pussy willow, fruit and all kinds of things to church on Easter Sunday to get them "blessed". She always wondered if they would "multiply" like the bread and fish in the Bible. Perhaps someday there would be enough bread to go around… Each of them had to eat three pussy willow buds and a slice of an egg. Everyone also took some of the newly blessed Holy water home.

The "Fronleichnam-Procession" had the entire town on its feet. It was the custom that the priest carried the "Monstranz" holding the "Holy Host" through the streets and fields – to bless the town and the fields that people were so dependent on. The houses were decorated with flower-garlands, all little girls that had white dresses would walk along in the endless rows of people – flower wreaths in their hair - singing and praying and chanting rosaries to the sound of the church bells. Diana never had a white dress. People were carrying flags and candles, branches and flower trellises adorning holy pictures and statues of Saints. Some of these "blessed" sprigs and flowers were taken home then; you would see them on doors and stables, and at the "Herrgott's Eck", the corner in the kitchen where the cross hung - as protection from sickness and disasters.

Diana's Holy Confirmation came one Sunday, and she had no sponsor. She wondered later where all their relatives were. Her mother practically begged a lady walking by as they were planting their garden the Saturday before, to sponsor her. She barely knew the lady. She lived a few villages away. She agreed. After church her sponsor bought her a "Weisswurst"- Hotdog on a roll. This was a rare meal. She also gave her a little cross on a thin chain. Years later Diana was able to visit her, and she would never forget the slice of bread she gave her with fresh churned butter and the glass of milk with butter flakes swimming on top.

There were very few events that were not religious in nature. There once was a fair in town and her parents let her go on the Ferris wheel, an experience she never cared to repeat. She remembered something resembling a puppet theatre in their school. It fascinated her so much that she forever after made puppet theatres out of paper and cardboard as a child and as an adult for her own children. A yearly event was "Fasching," a Mardi-Gras dance for adults just before the Lenten Holiday.

The "Federn-schleissen" (feather plucking) was a fun-social-working event of the women who would get together at one of the farmhouse kitchens and pluck chicken feathers, separating the down from the stems, to make featherbeds. They would talk, and laugh and dance. Their joys were very simple. Her mother rarely went anywhere; she was not the socializing type and shied away from gossip. However this was productive, because that's how they came to get a featherbed.

At gatherings like this, all the town's laundry was aired, and when all the gossip was exhausted, there were the stories about the dark sides. They had a life of their own - restless souls rising up from graves, ghosts at large, the wrath of god in form of fires and storms, curses, mystic objects, psychics and prophets, heaven and hell and purgatory…There was no end to these stories.

These occasions were probably the origin for much superstition that became mixed with religious beliefs, and reflected the suppressed and tortured minds of the times.

There was no Halloween. On New-Years Day or Eve they would dress up as the "Three Kings". A couple of her girlfriends and her would go from house to house singing the "Three Kings"- song, hoping that someone would feel sorry for them freezing outdoors and would invite them in for something hot to drink, perhaps some cookies. It happened a few times. It was always Diana that organized those things.

There was St.Nikolaus Day, the sixth of December, one of the many religious Holydays in Germany. This one was special, because St.Nickolaus was known to be a friend of children. On that day he was said to come in person- and sometimes he did -to reward "good" children with gifts and little things they could write a wish list for. It was a version of Christmas. The 24 /25 December was the more religious celebration of the birth of Christ with less emphasis on gift-giving. So, on St. Nickolaus Day, every hopeful child would set out a slipper the night before…

They had to get in good with St. Nikolaus, because it wasn't only he, but also his servant, Knecht Ruprecht, that would come around. He would announce his visit the night before with a clatter… He was known to discipline the bad boys and girls, and beat them with his chain. Diana never saw him, but other kids did, and they had the welts to prove it. He wore all black, a huge chain wrapped around his waist that would drag on the ground. Only to hear a clatter… was enough to scare the best of children. The fear of him did not allow her much joy and anticipation of St. Nikolaus. Diana never understood this, and later she wished they had just skipped the whole thing

Then there was the Rauchnacht, ("Smokenight"), on NewYears Eve, a custom that must have been somehow related to the Three Kings bringing gold, frankincense and myrrh to the Jesus Child. Every house had to be purified, after every corner and crack and cobweb was meticulously cleaned. Then her mother would bless the house with Holy water, and walk around every room with a pot of burning coals, sprinkled with myrrh, and this would give off smoke and an atrocious foreign smell. This ritual would chase away the evil spirits. A house that hadn't been "cleaned" this way was believed to house these spirits into the next year. Was she scared of these "spirits"!

There were stories about dead people that "couldn't rest", someone being "possessed by the devil", a "black dog", that was haunting and terrorizing their neighbor's family after the old man died…That dog could not be killed even after it was stabbed a dozen times. Their neighbor was a mean man, they said. They knew it. He would chase them kids off his property if they dared to look up at his cherry trees. The story was that there were strange things going on at this house, and this dog was really an evil spirit, or even the devil himself. They were not allowed to set foot on that property.

On their way to town they had to pass a cross on the side of the road, a memorial of someone who had died at that spot. They were scared to death to pass it after dark, because people swore that they saw eyes wandering around, watching that area. Their parents never really told them about those strange things, but they'd overhear them talking, and she was sure they believed them as well. She remembered her parents talking about coming home one day late at night, walking by that cross. A huge "black dog" stood in the road in front of the cross and would not let them walk past. They both stared at the dog and did not take their eyes off him as her father slowly bent down for a rock. As he raised his arm to throw it - right before their eyes in one instant, the dog disappeared. It sure spooked the children, and they were scared to walk past that cross for many years. Her mother would say: "Let's pray for the poor souls"…

This cross was still there.

There were stories about certain houses being haunted, about the "living dead" walking around there…One of their neighbors swore that their deceased relatives repeatedly moved heavy furniture around in their upstairs bedroom, so boisterous that the ceiling shook. When they ran upstairs and opened the door, it stopped – leaving scratches all over the floor and the furniture scrambled in the middle of the room. After they left, the spirits would continue. Someone hanged himself; they said that the devil made him do it...

Strange people, strange events…

There always was this feeling that they were vulnerable and defenseless against these evil forces at large, that they had no more control over them than anything else in their lives. They would try to hide in prayer as a refuge, a safe place…

Diana always wondered what she had to do to escape those "spirits" that haunted their town. Most of these events had a connotation of people having been bad, having done something wrong in their life and were now being punished in purgatory, not able to find peace. She supposed this religious and spiritual mentality played a role in keeping order in their town. It sure made an impression on her.

When she first saw the movie "Poltergeist" she found it very familiar. She thought the story must have originated in her hometown. There was so much "mystic" symbolism, so many customs and rituals, superstitions and "sayings", and she was not sure they didn't traumatize a small child's tender and fragile mind.

Then came Christmas! It was a miraculous time each year. Diana remembered it being warm at their house in every sense of the word, with an air of anticipation and wonder and hope. There was a feeling of comfort and safety protecting them from the cold world outside. Sometimes her sisters and brothers would come home and they would sing "Silent Night" together… They always had a fresh Christmas tree, cut down from the forest behind their house. They trimmed the tree with lots and lots of tinsel and a few glass ornaments, beautiful ones, "from Czechoslovakia," her mother would say every year, and homemade ornaments made from cookie dough, called "Lebkuchen". Some cookies had pictures of St. Nikolaus glued to them.

Diana felt some nostalgia thinking about the small candles in metal holders clipped to the branches. She would see the tiny joy and hope and excitement in their mother's eyes as she would carefully light them, and them – breathlessly watching them burn…and drip…and melt away…

One Christmas her mother was able to get some chocolate and cocoa butter and they made little chocolates. They had to cool the little molds in the snow, because there were no refrigerators. They hung some chocolates on the tree. They made a version of the "Hansel and Gretel" Gingerbread house. Presents were apples, nuts, a homemade doll, a toy made of wood, a hand knitted scarf or a hat, mittens and long stockings. Her sister said she once missed her little 4" doll about three weeks before Christmas, and looked for it everywhere. No one had seen it. There under the Christmas tree was her doll in a brand-new dress with seven layers of laces…and it was the best Christmas.

Diana remembered, one Christmas they had taken in a "fugitive". It was a secret. He lived in their cellar and never went out. He was Polish, they said. They were always hiding some people for a time in the cellar or in the attic "until they found another place to live"…

Later it occurred to her that he wasn't Polish at all, but Jewish.

Diana thought this man was surely an artist. He could carve things out of cheap wood like they had never seen before. They would come alive. He made her an airplane she never forgot. It had intricate details painted on it, and many funny little stars. She hung that on our Christmas tree with awesome appreciation of art. Her mother took it off the tree. She said the plane with the funny stars was not for anyone outside the family to see. It was one of the nicest things a stranger ever did for her. All of a sudden this man had left. He disappeared. He was a friend, and she could not understand why he didn't say "good-bye. She kept that airplane for a long time, and wondered about it…did he have dreams to fly away in an airplane?

She hoped he did before the SS found him.

They would go to midnight mass, Christmas night, all together. They would walk 3 miles, freezing like no one's business. They didn't notice. They were admiring the stars in the Christmas sky, the Christmas stars… It was such a holy night; they would shudder in reverence. Was there a star for them? Her mother believed in miracles.

One Christmas she got to sing the part of the Christmas Angel in church, she was 12 or so. She had to climb many steps to stand at the pulpit, which towered up above the congregation. She cringed with every step. She practiced just going up there 99 times. She had a pretty voice, but was so scared to sing in front of the whole town. It went well: "Fear not, for today is born the

Savior, Christ, the Lord…" The entire town was hanging onto every word. They sang, they prayed, they gave thanks, they thought they saw a star, a light, and a hope

One day Diana was visiting her oldest sister Carol with her mother. The 60-mile bus trip to Passau was horrendous, she vomited all the way there. Still in the end Diana remembered it fondly. There she saw things that were beyond them. Her sister treated her a little grown up; she'd give her a scarf or a piece of her clothes and she made ribbons for her hair. She even let her smell her cologne, it was"4711" Diana was very intrigued, she didn't care if that was vane. Her sister was pretty, she had beautiful long brown hair, and she knew what to do with her hair. Diana never did. She so admired her sister.

It was a hard life for her family as well for many years, they knew hunger and cold and despair. Diana remembered the stairway on the outside of the barn where they lived vividly, it seemed like it had 100 icy, wooden, deteriorated steps to their 2-rooms.

She had six children, and a very quiet husband. Somehow she seemed to have the most patience and balance of all of them. And she dared to sing through it all.

When Diana was 13 years old, her mother knitted a sky blue sweater for her. It had white stripes and crocheted tassels that tied at the neck, and it matched the colors of the Bavarian Flag. It was her most special Christmas present ever, and certainly the prettiest sweater she ever had. It was the last sweater her mother made for her. Everyone admired it. She even had a picture taken in it, and that was a rare occasion in itself. A camera was a real luxury. Her brother brought one home once. It took months to get the pictures developed. Her sister gave her that picture; she still had it.

Another Christmas her oldest brother made a dollhouse for her, inspiring her lifelong fascination with dollhouses. It had no roof, was divided into two rooms, and had two windows and a door that opened. Her mother made curtains and a bedspread and pillows, and a little crocheted rug, and three little dolls. Diana was sure her sister helped her, too. She remembered cutting up every scrap of fabric she could get a hold of into little "rugs" and "bedspreads" after that. They didn't have any of those luxuries at home. Her brother made wood furniture: a cupboard, table and chairs, beds and night table, and even curtain rods. It was the most precious thing Diana had ever seen in her little life. It was hidden under her sister's bed behind all kinds of boxes for several weeks while they worked on it. Diana found it before Christmas.

This was a milestone in her little life, because she still believed in the "Christkindl", (the Christ-Child), that brought gifts –like Santa Claus. She kind of figured out that her brother was working on this dollhouse. It caused her a dilemma. There still was a chance that there was such a thing as the Christkindl, and if so she thought it would punish her for snooping and take it back. So she couldn't tell for fear that it might be gone the next day. She couldn't risk losing it. The anticipation was so precious; she was elated every minute until Christmas. She would check every day it if was still there.

Diana never told anyone that she had found it, until she was long grown up. Her conscience was very fine-tuned. It would not let her forget it. The secret was sweet, though deep down she felt she had betrayed a trust. She had faked the surprise at Christmas, and the integrity of the present was somehow jeopardized. She had not lied, but it sure felt like it. Was this a precursor of what adults call deception? She thought this had to one of those milestones that form character.

There was a law above all law, it was ingrained in them from childhood on "to be what you are", true to yourself. To be real, no falsehood, no lies, no deception, no fakes. To be truthful and honorable at all times was the commandment that came before all others. Her parents had very little, but they had honor and pride and respect. The worst thing they could have ever done to them was dishonor them by being anything less than this "code of honor" warranted. "Don't bring us any shame" still rings in her ears. They would have defended the honor of their family to death. Most people felt that way. A handshake was the contract. You would never go back on your word. Your word was all you had. It was sacred. Honor was such a treasure, and it had to be earned.

One would understand that as a child getting caught in the smallest lie would earn her severe punishment – like "kneeling" on split logs, raw, split logs that you would use for firewood. Diana remembered it well. The length of time one would kneel was determined by the severity of the transgression.

She must have lied sometimes – or maybe talked back, which was another thing that could earn one this kind of punishment. In her mind, this was one of the hardest measures of discipline for children, not exclusive to their household either. Kneeling, spanking, the belt, the paddle, the ruler, the willow stick and other forms of punishment were totally normal in their times, and legal, the same or similar for all. She had a strong apprehension toward belts and belt buckles to this day. They used to say, "Wer die Rute spart, liebt seine Kinder nicht" ("If one is conservative with discipline, one does not love one's children." Diana and her sister later in life laughed about it, saying that their parents must have loved them a lot.

The worst thing was that they were never allowed to cry after they were punished. "Not a sound… not another sound…" their father would say. If they kept crying, they asked for more.

33

There was no time for crying, for pouting, for them to feel sorry for themselves. Correction was necessary. They were supposed to "take it like a man." Crying was a weakness. They could not afford to be weak.

As an adult, when disaster hit, Diana was not allowing herself to feel and cry and grieve and acknowledge pain either. She became accustomed to denying pain. She "held it in" until she burst – which was often not the best time for decisions or ultimatums… To know how "to push on" was the best she could do. It was a learned trait.

Diana had a lot of pride as a child. Her least favorite of all punishments was kneeling. At least, a spanking would have been over and done with. Besides the agony of kneeling, and the painful knees, one had to deal with the feeling of humiliation and self-recrimination. Her fear of the severe punishment and all the shame and humiliation that followed was probably what caused her to lie in the first place, she thought. How could she tell that she fell off the neighbor's cherry tree when she wasn't supposed to go over there to begin with! When her limp and the obvious bruise on her forehead gave it away, she had to face the consequences anyway. It wasn't too smart to deny that she had been playing with the neighbor girls again that she wasn't allowed to associate with – when she would bring home their head-lice as clear evidence every time. Eventually she learned to respect her mother's prediction as gospel that "the truth will always come out".

Sometimes she hated her parents for being so strict and severe. They said they did it for her own good. She felt angry and hurt sometimes, but she knew that she had no right to those feelings.

On top of it all – after kneeling for as long as she could stand it - she was too proud to say that she was sorry, and beg that she be allowed to get up. More humiliation than she could stand! For most kids this came easy. She asked some of her friends. Not for her. One stayed down there forever if one didn't say that, exactly that. Sometimes Diana knelt much longer than she had to. She remembered her parents saying that she was the most stubborn child they ever knew. It was generally thought that one had to break a stubborn spirit. Her parents did their best. For her the humiliation was worse than the pain of kneeling. Anyway, her spirit wouldn't break easily, a family trait! She still has a problem with making apologies.

Her nieces and nephews proudly told her later that she always was considered the rebel in their family and their hometown. They assured her that this was a compliment; it proved to them that anything was possible if one sets his mind on it.

However for a child an attribute such as pride was totally discouraged. The times they lived in demanded subordination. Diana just never was the cookie-cutter, ordinary, most obedient child. She always felt like breaking out of the norm, like her world wasn't big enough for her to breathe in. Sometimes she wanted to try to walk the edge or test the limits – like out on the furthest limbs of the cherry tree where the cherries were the sweetest but the bough was most likely to break. She always had big dreams in her little head. She was a "free spirit" that nothing throughout her life could quite destroy. However, a child had no liberties or choices in their world. Not even adults had choices.

There were many children in every household; five was probably the norm. There were too many mouths to feed everywhere. In her childhood times women seldom had children by choice, and it was obvious that they were a burden, a nuisance at best. It was certainly the consensus in their time that children had to be clipped and pruned and disciplined, to make them grow straight, so they would be strong enough to withstand the weathers of the war-ridden times, hard times. It hardened Diana. It made her strong. There was a mentality of enduring, at least among the poor; a mentality of being tough, prepare for the worst, master challenges, grin and bear. Children had to be prepared for this kind of world.

Then again Diana thought that sometimes the grownups must have liked kids anyway. Why else would they have hoisted them up to ride home on top of the hay wagon – might as well have been on top of the world – when they were exhausted after a long day's work in the farmers' fields? That was one of the best of her childhood memories. There wasn't much fun and humor and patience for kids. Most of the time the children would work right along with their parents in the farmer's fields. As soon as they could hold a tool or a rake they learned the facts of life: You work, you eat. It was normal for them to be working, planting potatoes, fertilizing, turning the hay, raking up rocks in the blasting hot sun… anytime the farmers needed help, and the family needed food. No one had ever heard of "child labor".

One cold winter day, there was another milestone in her life. She came home from school; all frozen from the three-mile walk, with icicles hanging off her clothes as usual. She told her mother that she felt all wet, and really didn't feel good. Mother looked at her, and helped her get her wet jacket and skirt off, never yielding to her petrified stare. Girls wore skirts at that time, no matter how cold it was. That day the woolen stockings, held in place at the thighs with rubber band often unsuccessfully, felt more itchy and sticky than usual. The icicles all the way up her stockings and the rest of her bottom were a bloody mess. She had no idea where she had hurt herself. It scared her half to death. "Oh", said her mother, "that's nothing. You got your period now. You'll get this every month like all girls do. It's a normal thing."

"This is a very private thing", she said, "and shouldn't be talked about". Like who would talk about it? Certainly not their teachers, nor did anyone else. Talking to other girls was no help, they knew as much as she did. It must be sinful anyway, that's why no one should talk about it. They didn't even know the right words for things like vagina, uterus, or such, much less what they were for. Sex education? Everyone would have been appalled by the mere word. This "secret" was hanging over Diana like a black cloud. Even into her adulthood she struggled with this. She felt so awkward. She was ashamed. She never talked to anyone about it. It felt dirty. In those times one had to wash the soiled pads by hand, of course, they were not disposable. There was no such fancy thing. She never skipped gym, she would not ever admit to anyone that menstrual cramps were killing her, besides the horrendous headaches she got along with them every time. There was no aspirin or any other relief. It was shameful to complain, especially about something so normal. Diana hated being a girl and afflicted with this awful predicament. Growing up became less desirable all the time. No one ever talked about the wonder of a woman's body, a woman's reproductive system, the miracle of birth…She cannot even explain how impoverished they were in so many ways. Diana wished that they could have ever seen an ultrasound of a baby!

It was just as well that they didn't know any different, because for them there were no choices.

III

TIMES   OF   WAR

It was war, they whispered. It was always war. Everyone knew it. No one said anything. No one dared to talk about it. Everyone was afraid to breathe a word. Even the one bus that came every day wasn't coming anymore.

People in their small town were in shock, quarantined in their homes, in disbelief, as the little life they knew, exploded around them. The SS descended on their neighborhood, their own people, but now their enemy. It was war.

Diana was only a child at the time of WWII. She was on the German side. She was a child. She had no choice. Was she a victim, too? She had not committed any crimes, nor had her family. They learned about the crimes of Auschwitz years after the fact. They were victims as well. Yet she carried the guilt and shame of her "Vaterland" on her shoulders all her life, an awesome burden for her, however minute a dot she was on the canvas of that war.

Today again she found herself lost in that dark tunnel of memories, a tunnel that led to nowhere. Angrily she fought back her tears, a useless, attempt to change, to affect, to prevent an inevitable outcome.

Could anyone ever mend the remnants of destruction, or count the victims, the victims on all sides, victims intended and targeted as well as "casualties" of war, the innocent, the children…some dead, some still living…some no one will ever know… To this day Diana found it hard to sleep with the thought of leaving her children to a world capable of such violence. She realized that no one "wins" a war. Ruins don't sing praises of victory or defeat. The stigma of World War II will rest on German shoulders forever.

She was on the German side. No wonder she often felt like hiding her German heritage later in her life.

All her life she never talked about these things. She still shuddered at the thought of them. She would pretend to her children that she was just ignorant of the War {and immune to the pain}. She never talked about war, never read history books nor watch a war movie on television. She closed her mind to all reminders.

There was a reason. She had her own story. It was only a glimpse at the war time from a different angle, from the eyes of a German child that was there, in the middle of it. It was the irony she struggled with, the irony of having to live in fear of the German Gestapo, and praying for the Americans to rescue them from their own people.

Diana dared to talk about those things now, many years later, or even write about them – as she finally stood on high ground, secure, safe enough to think that her life wouldn't shatter around her anymore. Could it? She was never sure. As she was writing this she realized that tears were welling in her eyes, tears, those precious tears long overdue…She had barely opened the door to her life.

There was war, they said…There was always war.

Diana was a very sensitive child in such a harsh world, and the traumatic events of the war times had a devastating impact on her tender and vulnerable little life. She always felt her own pain and fear and hopes, and everyone else's around her, too. She would always fly high and fall hard – without a net or a lifeline. The experience of the war rolled over her like a tidal wave, and left a lot of broken pieces…

She was eight years old. She heard the war drums of the SS soldiers for many years later, as they were parading through the town then. She remembered the days when they were marching past their house, surrounding their house – stomping, crushing the frozen ground. She would close her eyes and ears and pretend they were horses.

Then they were not marching by. They were stationed around their house for days, weeks, endless weeks… They set up camp right under the old cross in the middle of the three birch trees next to their house, the cross that for ages had humbled people to bend their knees and cross themselves when walking by… From their kitchen window looking out onto their neighbor's higher ground the soldiers looked ten times bigger and scarier to her than they were. For years, in her nightmares, she heard the rhythm of them marching by. Nightmares were a normal thing for her; she thought everyone had them. She knew her mother did. When she dared to look out of their kitchen window once or twice, she saw the boots – and long after, the boots…big almighty boots. They seemed at least as scary as the uniform, the rifle hanging from the shoulders... That far up she didn't even dare to look. She just saw the boots. They represented everything she feared, so much power, that it was paralyzing... She remembered the sunlight reflecting off the buckles, piercing her eyes… She remembered shivering in bed at night listening to the sound of the boots crushing the snow with threatening determination, just a few feet from her window. She remembered trying to put faces on those boots that belonged to familiar people, guys she knew…in an attempt to lessen he fears of the impending certainty of their fate.

It was absolute law to stay clear of the windows and doors in the first place, and she should have listened. Of course her mother was trying to shield them and protect their home with her life. She was a child, and as frightened as she was, she just had to dare and look out once in a while – with a glimmer of hope that it was not as bad as it seemed or as they said. She was desperately trying to be brave and courageously adult for her mother, who certainly needed her, since she was the only one home with her most of the time.

Diana realized later, after her sister reminded her, that the SS were not the first troops that marched past their house. It wasn't the first time Diana had heard these drums, and felt the rhythm of war. This is why the impressions were so deep.

When she was 3 years old (1939), as the German troops were going to invade Czechoslovakia – they marched past their house with all the artillery of war, Half-tracks, troop carriers, and trucks. They marched past their house, located on the main road, the only road to the border of Czechoslovakia – day and night, thousands of them – in an endless mass of boots pounding to the beat of the war drums. Her sister said that their house rumbled and shook - their hearts, too, she was sure.

The troops set up camp in every house of their town then for several weeks, until negotiations made Czechoslovakia surrender.

Her sister remembered it well. She told her that even though their people were shaken by the surprise invasion, they felt sorry for the soldiers who were totally exhausted. As they were marching by, there was this little girl running along in the ditch on the side of the road – her sister – with a pitcher of water that they passed around and drank while keeping step, to the very last drop. She'd run back home again, and have mother fill it up again, and again, and run along again. As an adult when she was living in Munich, her sister ran into an older man that told of his war experiences, recalling the time they were invading Czechoslovakia, marching for weeks and weeks… "And there was this little girl", he said, "running alongside the road with a pitcher of water…"Diana's sister. That was Elli!

Later the Russians drove the Germans out of Czechoslovakia again, back across the border and through their town. Most troops were killed; many wounded. The men that returned from the war looked ashen, translucent, broken in body and spirit. You didn't have to ask. Their sunken eyes told what horrors they'd seen. Diana remembered the uniforms with war emblems and medals, the war caps, the boots, the rifles and these sunken eyes…She was afraid of them. Some men were sent home in wooden boxes, some were forever "missing", which prolonged the uncertainty and sorrow. She remembered so many coffins…all those wooden crosses…so many people wearing black clothing for years…The cemetery was a very familiar place for them. She remembered wondering as a small child why some people, especially the ones in fresh graves, had only a wooden board as a grave marker with their name on it, while others rested behind big stones with angels sitting on them. It didn't seem fair. There were many people dying in their town. They would be laid out on a board at their house in the living room (there were no funeral parlors). After they were buried that board was used as the marker on the grave.

She recalled these things from her earliest childhood, from three or four years of age. That was their world. Everything was all about war: going to war, someone "fell" in the war, waiting for someone coming home from the war…It seemed as though there always were soldiers around and drums and war songs, and people hiding out in their cellars – when she was a little girl. It was always war. She was always cold and hungry. She knew no different.

So it was still war when she was eight years old…it was World War II, going on forever….

Only now they were SS troops that surrounded their house, their own town's people, yet their enemies. Diana remembered listening to the sound of their boots - trotting by, trampling their lives…

All of their fathers were gone. During most of this time there was not a man in town. Either they had to join the SS, or they had to flee and hide in order not to get shot by them. Anyone that didn't agree with Hitler's philosophy or stepped out of line, was arrested, and not seen again. Her brothers and sisters were much older than she. They were living and working away in other towns, and could only come home occasionally. Only her brother Jo never came home; he was dead or "missing", they always said. Her mother had to worry about all of them, too, and could not protect them.

They did not know if her older brother was arrested as well. He had just come back from the French-German war, serving in the German Army on the Western Front. They said that he was not much of a soldier. He did not want to shoot a rifle, or kill a fly. He was more interested in making friends with the French enemies. He told them of the miracle that happened to him in that war. As he returned to the base with supplies one day, he realized that all the troops were gone. A sixth sense told him to run to the bomb shelter. He ran, and made it down the stairway as a bomb hit the shelter and killed the hundreds of men in it and around the entire area. He, in the doorway, was the only survivor. He attributed that to their mother's prayers. He survived the war and it did not break his sprit. He always had a guardian angel.

Diana remembered him singing and whistling and skipping around on scaffoldings of buildings. He taught her to whistle. He loved life, loved his family, loved motorcycles and his guitar. It was therapy for the family every time he was around, everyone would sing old songs together. Diana's mother would always say:" Come on in and stay where you hear singing; bad people don't sing."

At this time there was not much to sing about. It was war all over, they said. Diana remembered it was very cold and they didn't have much wood for their stove, the only heat source they had for the whole house. She thought the cold was the reason why they had to wear all the clothes they owned to sleep at night – including their coats, mittens, hats and shoes. Later she learned that they never knew from night to night if they didn't suddenly have to run; if their house would burn down, like others had in town, or they were being bombed. They heard explosions and sirens, and the night sky was red, they said, from burning cities…There were airplanes in the sky, something they had never seen in their lives before. Some people said that bombs were raining on the cities on the other side of the mountains…

It was war, they said. That's all Diana knew.

She thought that she felt no more scared and lost and poor than other kids, and she was used to being hungry and cold. She saw no friends during that time, because no one was allowed to leave the house. There was no school for a while, either. All the young boys had to enroll in the Hitler-Youth group. They were tired of the drills, the sirens and parades and the war songs anyway. It was too dangerous for the kids to walk three miles to school. Most of the time the SS had barricaded the road. They felt like prisoners. Her mother was afraid to leave the house because the SS had already threatened to set it on fire. She had to stay watchful day and night. She constantly walked around the house, checking windows and doors, listening and praying…

Neighbors would sneak around, and the news was not good.

Diana did not know that there was a tomorrow. She said her prayers at night, and did not expect to wake up in the morning. "If I should die before I wake…" She never taught her children this prayer. It gave her the chills ever after.

It was freezing outside. They froze inside their house. The SS marched by, huffing and puffing and cursing, demanding that her mother let them come inside to warm up. Her mother would not hear of it. She would yell at them: "You idiots, go home if you are cold." She would shut the door in their faces. This stuck in Diana's mind to this day. She was scared of them, she hated them, she did not want them in the house, of course, but she had never heard her mother being so cruel. She'd take in a sick animal and nurse it back to health. She wouldn't step on a cricket or a worm. She felt sorry for a mouse that the cat dragged in. Diana did not understand. Much later she heard them talking about it. These soldiers were their own people at war with them. Their own neighbors, village boys, her sister's boyfriends were now "The SS" and did what they were told by the "Fuehrer". Diana understood little what that meant.

Much later she realize that they did not either.

Many a young boy was made an SS soldier overnight. Most had never worn a boot before, or even seen a uniform, much less held a rifle…yet they were loyal to the "Vaterland" and willing to die for it.

The question came to her mind: Why the German soldiers so blindly followed commands? How could they do such unspeakable things, even to their own people? Were they not able to distinguish right from wrong? However, every German child was raised not to question authority. They all were taught that loyalty as five-year olds already – marching like little robots in the Hitler parades, drilling war songs, crying "Heil Hitler" and "Sieg Heil". They were taught that loyalty to the "Vaterland" was an absolute duty above any other – the loyalty that turned brother against brother, children against their parents - innocent little children preyed on to give away a secret…the where-abouts of their parents…all in the name of the greater loyalty. What a cruel world!

The reason the SS soldiers were staking out Diana's house was that it stood on a small hill from where they could see a long way, at least thirty miles. They were watching the road, the only road in and out of our town. It invisibly wound through the forest toward a clearing, called "Kreuz," (that was what they had their eyes on) and it ultimately led to the big city, Passau, which was equal to civilization. There they knew what was going on, people said. The rumors were that the "Americans" were coming at any time. The SS were looking for them. Did they want to disappear just in time, or would they shoot at the Americans? In Logan they were setting up to ambush them, people said. Their house surely would be in the line of fire. No one knew what the SS might do; they weren't considered to be too smart, and everyone also knew that they were ruthless. The adults were praying for their rescue. The German people would welcome the Americans with open arms hoping that they would save them from their own people, at least what was left of them. However the SS would have shot them if they knew. So everyone stayed put and waited...

Occasionally someone would come by and whisper something, drop a few words. No one trusted his neighbor or his brother; you couldn't be seen talking to anyone and everyone was considered a spy. Newspapers weren't coming. All information was controlled - what little there was. There was severe punishment threatened for listening to foreign radio stations. Not to worry - only a couple of people had radios in town. The time for television had not yet come for them either.

The pastor had a radio. He even found a Radio-station that did not only broadcast the German doctrine. He was very devoted to their town, the town he had lived in all his life. Somewhere in his Sunday sermon he would weave a disguised message to alert and warn the Parishioners. Someone then informed on him, and the SS promptly came right after church to arrest him. The men that were left in town met secretly at a "Bierstube" late at night, trying to make sense out of it, and plan strategy. What could they do, but wait and see?

The bus was still coming most of the time, and the people that got off were talking. They told stories too horrible to believe. Someone was at the train-station in the city. They said they saw a train full of people being transported to a "camp" – people with terribly sad eyes. No one got off that train, they said. No one really knew what a "camp" was. There were many rumors, and no one knew what to believe, or what was going to happen. Everything was out of control. The news came slowly and secretly, but eventually it came. Someone had heard that all the important and outspoken people in town – anyone that was somebody – had been arrested, the Principal, their Pastor, teachers, etc. Their principal? Their pastor? It was true. He was arrested by the SS and dragged off – accused of sabotage. When word got around, most pastors in the area fled or were arrested then.

Their principal had educated several generations in town. Everyone knew him, loved and trusted him. Now he was an SS official with the highest honors, and most people were very skeptical about that, some wouldn't even send their children to school. However when he didn't agree with the later philosophy of the "Fuehrer", the Regime discharged him dishonorably and took away his teaching license. Then he was arrested because he refused to replace the crosses in the classrooms with Hitler's picture. Even after he was gone, the parents would come to school in protest, hanging the cross back up, and taking Hitler's picture down, over and over.

When the bronze bells of all the churches were confiscated to be molten down for war materials, the people were outraged. Was this not a sacrilege, a sign that their faith and their values were trampled on, their hopes thrashed, their beliefs traded for the pride in their "Vaterland?" One should know the significance of the church bells ringing in Europe. They ring in the day in every village, they ring in every hour, the Baptisms and the Funerals, every occasion from the beginning to the end of everyone's life…The war machine had not only molten down the bells but the spirit of the people. After the war one church in Callen was the only church around with bronze bells, because the pastor lied to the authorities – as he later confessed – telling them that their bells were of steel, not bronze.

Hitler had done a good job of convincing the German people that he was their salvation. They had been so tired of hunger and slavery and hard times, they were desperate enough to follow a leader promising better times. Better times? He had started out with many promises for the suppressed country: a better economy than Germany had seen, work and education. Streets were being built. There were programs for youths, daycare for poor children, even camps for undernourished kids, such as both her sisters. There was home-health-care for the old and for mothers after childbirth. There was family counseling, and the state paid 20.00 DM per child to families with more than three children. There was food and medicine for the poor. Any social services had been foreign to these people. This is how Hitler won over the trust of the German people, for a while, for too long a while…

Many things were certainly "red flags" for their religious town that Hitler was trouble. Now people said: "The power has gone to his head! He is playing God"! Her mother had long made up her mind about him. She said that changing the cross into a swastika was a sacrilege. No good could come of that!

Someone said that Hitler was going to breed a "pure race", and do away with all the unfit. In fact, her sister said the kids were examined in school for blue eyes and blond hair, and the naïve children thought it was a game and were proud if they were blue-eyed and blond...

Her mother said God would punish him. Diana didn't find any comfort in believing that "God's mills mill slowly, but surely", as she always said.

Many people didn't trust Hitler from the start, but they would wait and see… What were the people of a small village going to do to stop the war machine? They were Victims of it themselves. What choices did they have? People were confused, scared, appalled. Some started to act up. Some people refused to raise their arm to the "Fuehrer"in the "Heil- Hitler" salute. That's when the last of the men in town were arrested, as most were already gone. So they fled into the high forests where they could not easily be found. There were no roads in those forests where the jeeps of the SS could follow. They had to get help. They had to save their families from the SS. The Americans were their only hope. Some of the men were shot before they could get far enough away. They were working their way toward "Kreuz" on foot and trying to stay out of sight, weaving through forests for miles and miles, hoping that they would meet up with the Americans before long. The SS were feared and scorned. They would shoot at random. They set houses on fire, if they did not like someone. They sure did not like them, Diana knew that their house was a target anyway, because its location was ideal for a lookout, and her mother…she was not very cooperative. She really believed they would arrest her mother or drag her away… some of the SS had already warned her sister to tell her mother to "cooperate" or they would shoot her.

People in town were hiding and burying their goods, food and anything precious of what little they had. The SS were stealing and looting and vandalizing everywhere. Who was going to stop them? Everything was fair game.

They did not have any place to hide anything. Just before her father had to leave he had an idea. He took up the wood floor in their kitchen at night. They dug out a big hole, and carried dozens of buckets of dirt out in the stable. This was done very secretly, and by oil lamp, so they would not arouse suspicion. There were SS spies everywhere, and people were reported if there was anything unusual going on. The SS seemed like God. Somehow they knew everything. Keeping secrets from the SS was considered a crime. Everyone was terrified. They felt they were spies – hiding their own things!

They had little to hide. Diana knew there were their featherbeds (they wore all their clothes to sleep anyway), some dishes, linens, clothes, their clock, their sewing machine, some knickknacks, a pair of her father's leather shoes and the little food they had. Her father then put the boards back, and the floor looked just the same. Then came the shocker: As they walked over the hollowed-out area of the kitchen floor, it sounded different. Was it just because they knew that there was something buried down there? She knew her father's heart missed a few beats; he was so disappointed and exhausted. They kept walking across it a hundred times, but it stayed the same. It sounded hollow. So they hoped that no one would come in the house, and dare walk around. A few days after that their father had to leave and hide from the SS, and mother and her were left with their secret. The SS were still surrounding their house. Her mother was firm. She wasn't leaving. Where would they go anyway?

Then came the visits from the SS official. He was decorated with badges and medals all over. He had authority. They didn't know him. Her mother was forced to let him in the house. She always made Diana disappear into the stable, where they had their precious cow – their livelihood –, which actually was some comfort to her then, thank God. Her other hiding place was behind the drapes of their arched doorway between kitchen and bedroom. She remembered sitting motionless on the floor other than biting her nails. The harassment her mother endured from that official went on for hours and days. She'd hear her mother like she had never heard her before shouting and pleading and crying and swearing the wrath of God down on him. She was like a tigress, fiercely trying to protect her own. He would get very agitated and angry, that General, – and pace the floor – pace the floor… and every step would echo in Diana's ears.

He wore big boots. She could tell every time he stepped on the first board over the hole under the floor. It was like a torture listening. She counted his steps backwards and forward every time. She cringed and prayed that he would not notice it. She understood the consequences. People were arrested for less than this. To the SS this would be deliberate distrust, an act defying authority, and hiding anything from the SS was an offense in itself. If you were caught hiding some people or contributing to it, you were hauled off along with them. Everything was controlled and censured. Everyone avoided mention of Hitler's name, like one wouldn't mention the devils'.

Diana often wondered what her mother did to that SS official, because she realized that the Hitler Regime didn't mess around with common people. Perhaps she got to him somehow. She wondered why he wasted so much time with her. Usually people that resisted the SS were just taken away…Perhaps he was investigating if she was Jewish or they really wanted possession of their house badly. She must have had a guardian angel. Really, as often as this official came to their house, and paced that floor, he must not have been too smart if he didn't notice the hole under the kitchen floor. Talk about suspense for a child! Of course, her mother admitted to her later that her heart had pounded with his every step, too.

Long after that Diana had nightmares of that arrogant man, his omnipotent boots walking over their own bodies…Long after the war she hated every man that wore boots…

During some of this man's visits she would hide in the stable. She remembered feeling cold and stiff from fear more than the cold. She would sit in front of her cow "Scheckei", and warm her hands on the breath from her nostrils. She couldn't hear everything from the stable, which was worse. It made her feel more helpless and anxious and lost. Her mother was in there - alone with this horrible man, and she couldn't help her if anything happened, if she would be hurt or taken away or the house set on fire and she wouldn't know when it was time to run or where to go. She was always ready for anything. She figured it was better for this man not to know that there was a child around, it would have made her mother even more vulnerable. So she would listen with her ear pressed against the door. She heard enough to know that her mother appealed to that man's every sense of decency, religious and social conscience (as if he had any). She tried to just wear him out.

After a while even Diana sensed that the situation had become more threatening than even her courageous mother could handle. It was then, that she and Diana took their cow one very early dawn so they couldn't be seen and walked it over the hill through the forest to her uncle's house – about 3 miles away – because his place was isolated, way off the path, and less endangered. They had to save their cow! This was a traumatic journey for her. Her mother was trying to hide her tears and desperation. If they could only save their cow, their family's most valued commodity! She believed that they would never go home again. They had nothing left there anyway.

They did. Turned right around and went home, another three miles. It was evening when they neared the clearing where their house stood. They couldn't believe their eyes! They saw smoke! The SS had set their house on fire! Her mother grabbed her hand and pulled her behind her, they flew! They entered from the back, at the stable. Diana couldn't remember very clearly what happened next. She saw her mother climbing up to the attic where they had stored hay and feed for the cow and all that was in flames. She saw her mother walking into the flames… Somehow with the help of a miracle she put out the fire, and came down again. She was indestructible! If Diana feared anything more than boots, it was flames. She had seen many of them. Her mother walked through fire, and put it out. How she admired her!

The next day, or very shortly after that Diana's sister came home. She was housekeeper and Nanny for the forest ranger family in an adjoining town. He was arrested, too, they said, but there was talk that he might be involved with the SS .Her mother didn't trust the situation anymore, so she insisted that her sister quit and stay home now. Her sister didn't understand. She felt she needed to be responsible to the Ranger Family with five children and didn't want to desert them. She pleaded with her mother to let her stay. Her sister had no idea how desperate their situation was at home.

"What's this ax doing here at the front door"? Her sister took the ax and put it back in the stable into the tool rack. She wore their mother's apron while she was cooking dinner, and suddenly discovered the large pocket in front of the apron filled with pepper.

Their mother sat them down and there came the discussion that would really shake them up, and none of them would ever forget. Their mother said that she felt things were totally out of control. She felt that she could not protect them any longer. She said that she wishes the fires of hell would swallow up the entire Hitler Regime. She said they waited too long… She said the world was coming to an end… She hoped that their father would come back. She wished that the Americans would come and drive the SS out of there. She was desperate. This was incredible to her sister. Eleven years older than Diana– and gullible and innocent at nineteen, she was arguing with mother: "These guys are my friends, they aren't bad guys, I went to school with them, they are just misguided as SS soldiers. They are freezing out there…"

Their usually calm and controlled mother was incensed! She yelled: "Do you know – I guess you do not – that every girl you went to school with, and many of their mothers have been raped and brutalized by the very same, your friends, our very own people? They set our house on fire, our very own people! Did you know that all the men in town were driven away, or arrested, or shot? That the SS were shooting at them on sight? Yesterday they were lined up just twenty yards from our house, shooting with machine guns at the edge of the forest where our men were suspected to be hiding. Anything that moved, they shot at. There are people in town just disappearing, entire families. They lived here all their lives. You went to school with these kids".

Her sister didn't know anything. None of their family knew that these families were Jewish, or why being Jewish should be different. They had no idea where they disappeared to, or why. Some people were sending packages and collecting clothes and blankets and food for some that had moved to Poland or somewhere (packages they would never receive). Their mother said she heard that Hitler wanted to eliminate Jewish people. That's why they were hiding out in everyone's attic and cellar! Some had to wear yellow star patches on their arms for identification. They reminded Diana of the little stars on her airplane. It could be them tomorrow. Who knows, maybe they were Jewish and didn't know it. It seemed that the Gestapo just suspected people for any reason, and labeled them. People just disappeared. One never knew who might inform on you. She went to school with a retarded boy that was dragged out of his house in the middle of the night by the SS, and no one could find out what happened to him. He had Epilepsy, and they all felt sorry for him.

"I'll tell you", her mother said, "the ax stays by the door, and so does the pepper in the pocket. Anyone of them coming in the door from now on gets a hand full of pepper in their eyes, and their head chopped in two." That sobered her sister. She stayed home. Now their mother had to worry about her under their own roof.

Fear was such a big part of their lives, it consumed them, they expected no different. It was like a vise that it would take a lifetime trying to escape. According to her mother and several "prophets" from the bible and such, the world would be coming to an end soon anyway. It was imminent. They were watching for signs in the sky, not that they knew what they were, but the skies had never been red before. Diana remembered on some of the scariest nights all of them huddling on the floor – saying rosaries together – to drown out the noises outside, and their fears…to keep them safe from the evil forces at large…

Sometimes Diana was surprised to wake up in the morning. She couldn't remember a tear from this time, not a tear of hers, or a tear of anyone else. Everyone was tough. Everyone was strong. There was no time to cry. There never was a time to cry. She never expected tomorrow. She didn't think anyone did. Except her mother.

The role of the woman their town changed forever. With all the men gone, the women were left to fend for themselves. They took over – worked the farms, tended the animals and birthed the calves, chopped the wood, carried the full load…they managed their businesses and their large families. Their anger and desperation prompted courage and survival skills they never knew they had, defying rape and horror and disasters. They were tough and industrious and smart. Had they finally earned the respect of even their own men, the respect of society? Many men never returned after the war, and from then on at least it was no longer a disgrace and a stigma for a woman to be alone, like it had been in those days.

One morning, the middle of May 1945, the SS were gone. As Diana looked out the window she saw big tanks coming down the street, big brown tanks with canons, trucks packed with soldiers pointing their guns at what? Resistance? They moved so quietly, cautiously, peacefully in a slow caravan right past their house. She remembered sweeping the floor, the dustpan in her hand… She yelled for her mother. It took her only a second to know. She cried: "The Americans! The Americans"! She grabbed a sheet off the bed, ran upstairs and waved it frantically out the attic window, afraid that they wouldn't see the "white flag" and shoot at them, afraid that they might see them as enemies. They might think they were hiding SS, or were unwilling to surrender?

The first week the Americans were now patrolling their streets, and there was a curfew in the evening. American soldiers followed her sister into their house one day, and then they came more often. They were not afraid of the Americans despite the fact that they couldn't understand their language. They were not threatening like the SS had been, but friendly, peaceful and even funny. Sometimes they brought chocolate and chewing gum. Their mother invited them for a sparse meal. They trusted them.

It was the first joyful time Diana remembered having for a long time. People were actually walking out in the street again. People were talking again…some were waving, crying, cheering…

The American Soldiers gave them life back again. They didn't have to be afraid anymore – of their own people…No one was ever happier to have lost a war. Their fathers came home. School started – some of their teachers came back, some didn't. The cross was back on the wall of their classroom, a symbol of victory even though they had lost the war, they said. Some of their friends never came back. Someone said, they moved away, or were "relocated". Diana did not know what the whole story was, for years. They didn't know of the concentration camps and all the horrors. They were victims, too. It had happened somewhere else, on the other side of the mountains, a few hundred miles away, which might have been countries away. They had never even seen the nearest city, 60 miles from them. Diana was nine years old that December.

They were surprised to learn that a few of their town's people they would have never suspected, were now being arrested, because they had been members of the "Third Reich" all along

– out of fear of losing their job, or their life… Some people were questioned about what their position had been during the Hitler times. Some people left town now. When would the war be over?

Hundreds of refugees, mostly women and children, from Schlesien and the surrounding countries descended on their village, on every household, every day – bombed or driven away from their homes with nothing but the clothes on their back. There wasn't enough food to feed their own families. It was amazing that there was enough compassion and bread to go around…Somehow they were sheltered and fed and funneled through their border-town to surrounding areas.

Diana's family had people living in the attic again, a mother with her grown-up son…He kissed her once when she was home alone. She did tell her mother, even though she was very much ashamed and confused. The next thing she knew – they were gone! It was never mentioned again.

The living conditions were of catastrophic proportions. The bitter poverty, hunger and housing are hard for anyone's standards to comprehend. There was no work for so many more people, and there was little in the stores to buy. People would barter anything for food.

Diana thought AMERICA must be heaven. During some of the worst war times, she remembered getting a big package from their mother's cousin living in America. This happened at least three times. The contents of these packages were totally "out of their world". There were beautiful dresses, coats, skirts, belts, blouses…they dare touched the exquisite fabrics.

When Diana went to fabric stores later in her life, she still enjoyed "touching the fabrics", and she saw them opening these packages.

There were shoes that would always fit someone in the neighborhood. She would think of these shoes sometimes later as she read the Cinderella story to her children. There were long white and red lacy gloves, like nothing they had ever seen before, a hat with a scarf attached, jewelry – earrings (unheard of) and bracelets her sister was dying to wear. There were some baby cloth that her doll wore ever after, bonnets and bows and frilly little girls' dresses that she showed off her little niece wearing to church at her next visit. There were little sachets of soap and bath oil…there was dry milk, and rice, and raisins…If her cousin in the USA only knew what treasures the little knickknacks were to them that she probably gladly disposed of. Diana remembered her mother sitting over a long letter to her – a thank-you from the bottom of her heart, she was sure. Diana was wondering and dreaming of this fairyland…

People used to say that a space in your front teeth indicated that you were going far away some day. How she wished! Diana had a wide space between her upper front teeth. There were no braces in their time, not even a dentist in town. Most people didn't' know a toothbrush nor a toothpaste. She remembered her father pulling people's teeth with a pair of pliers and no anesthetics while her brother had to hold their head. She would run away and hide, because she couldn't stand hearing someone scream. She was always embarrassed and self-conscious about that ugly space between her front teeth, but now she thought of it as a positive. She believed in this superstition. She wouldn't mind going far away, far away, across the rivers and oceans… Would the boots and the nightmares follow her?

The German people loved the American soldiers. They were everyone's heroes. People would talk about them in awe, about their kindness and generosity. It was the general consensus that the Americans loved children. The German people were not accustomed to much kindness coming from anywhere. Life was raw, people were poor; no one gave them anything. You worked - you ate, that was it, (if there was work). Only a few farmers were a little better off, but most of them were too greedy to share; that included relatives. You took from no one, and there wasn't much envy, either. Everyone just tried to survive. Charity was not acceptable. You had your pride. You earned what you had. No one could take away your pride…

The American soldiers were so different. The American Soldiers seemed to have no ulterior motives. Their generosity was pure and simple. There was no shame in accepting. It was just there for the taking. Eventually they all accepted it. They just kept coming, and giving, and smiling, and they wanted nothing in return. Also, people were desperate to believe in some good, especially after living among the SS traitors.

There were also some rumors of cruel things the Americans supposedly did. Someone said that they arrested and even shot some of the Nazis – not that the town would care; (they must have deserved it), and no one really wanted to believe it. There also were whispers about a noticeable amount of "big bellies" among German girls a few months later, not to speak of the same proud mothers showing off their babies, African-American babies, Caucasian babies, war babies…

The first African-American people they ever saw were some American soldiers. They were kind and sociable, and everyone loved them. They knew no prejudice.

There were parties in town. The soldiers played American music. Diana saw her parents dancing. She could not believe her eyes. Her sister, yes, she was always skipping and dancing around the house, but never her parents. She remembered looking at her mother's legs, her feet moving lightly across the floor. She could not believe they were the same legs that carried home haystacks three times her size on her back from miles in the forest– just yesterday…There must be a reason to celebrate, if she danced today…

Diana attributed everything good that happened from that time on to the American soldiers. Nothing so good had ever happened to them before. She remembered how the kids would run behind their jeeps. They wouldn't shoo them away. They would compete for their attention. Often they would stop, or toss them a Hershey Bar or a package of Wrigley's Chewing Gum, the likes of they had never seen or tasted. They would collect every cigarette butt they dropped. They would take them home to their fathers, who would roll their own cigarettes with them.

Hunger was a reality in their lives. They knew no different - until now! Diana would never forget the huge kettles of soup that the American soldiers provided and served to them at school, every day for months to come. They all had their little cups hanging from their backpacks that they gave them. Every-day at lunchtime, every child was given a big ladle of soup: Split pea with ham, or tomato-rice or chicken-noodle, or rice pudding with raisins, and the best: thick hot chocolate with rice … She can still taste each one of them.

All these wonderful things happening fueled Diana's vivid and fertile imagination. It was around that time that she learned to dream… She knew that it wasn't reality. She dared to dream of another life, to be someone else but her…She dreamed of a land of plenty, of beautiful things, and miracles – that of course only happened in "Once-upon-a-time" fairytales. They had the "grim" Brothers-Grimm Storybooks. Most of their stories were scary. They identified with them. They were written for their times.

Somehow, there was hope after the war was over. People somehow cleaned up the rubble, gathered the pieces of what was left of their lives…They started mending the fences and stacking up brick by brick… rebuilding their shattered hopes, their shattered homes and lives and battered minds. Every hand was needed, be it a woman's or child's…every remnant of dignity, every prayer of hope, the last and the best of what everyone could give. People couldn't rest, they were driven to work. Someone asked: "Was it only the need to put some normalcy back in their lives that drove them with such urgency to work, to clean up the mess of the war?" Or were they really trying to clean every reminder of it out of their minds, the sooner the better?

Normalcy? What meant "normal" to them was that their family was almost whole again after their father came home. Almost that their mother's prayers were less desperate. What was normal to them was that they had milk again because their cow was back in their stable, and that they could sleep with their feather beds again that had been buried under the kitchen floor that they didn't have to be afraid anymore… Normal was that they could play outside and that they could climb cherry trees again… Normal was that they had their everyday chores to do, and their mother had no worries anymore other than to put food on the table. Normal was that their neighbor's rooster woke them in the morning along with the old familiar noises of people working, tending their animals…the sounds of saws and axes and the smell of manure in the neighborhood. Normalcy was, to see the hustle and bustle of the women working in their gardens, planting everything that might grow, hanging laundry, shining their windows again, scrubbing and washing away the dirt and the ghosts of the war... What was normalcy?

When did the war stop? Did it stop? They were still starving. There were no alternatives to their way of life. It was a hard fact. They were still just as poor, but they had a taste of something that let them believe that there was a tomorrow after all.

There was hope. Their people knew how to work. Oh, did they know how to work! They were industrious. They would not give up. They would rebuild. And while the world watched, the German spirit rose up from the rubble and started rebuilding…

There was hope. Diana clung to that lifeline. She learned her first English song from the soldiers: "You are my sunshine"…She sang it day and night. She started taking "lessons in English" from an old lady who knew a few words, like "How do you do? I am fine". She wanted to be able to talk to the soldiers. She dreamed of them taking her away to this country of theirs. A whole New World opened for her.

Perhaps there were castles and princesses and miracles out there. Perhaps you could escape the trolls and witches and dragons, and boots…Perhaps there were choices and possibilities…There must be something out there. Something good, something different. Diana really believed that. Freedom she did not know.

IV

<u>A   LEGACY</u>

"Without your honor…you have nothing. "Her father.

His family name dates back to Roman times… Records show that his ancestors were of Royal decent. Born in 1896 – her father was a most honorable man, a man of great pride and dignity. "If you don't have your honor, you have nothing," he often said – something they never forgot. Diana remembered pictures of him from World War I. He stood tall, and walked like the General all his life. However, when she was little, he would let her stand on his feet and dance with her, rock her on his foot when she caught him sitting down, or run his hand over her head – sometimes...

She never knew her grandparents. Most were already dead at her time. She faintly remembered being taken to her grandfather's house before he died - a dark room, and people sitting around whispering, and a spit-box at the side of his bed in their big farm kitchen. They had a raven that would sit on a pole above the kitchen door. He surprised people that came in, especially those people he did not like, by swooping down onto their shoulders or head. They talked about that raven stealing jewelry and watches and shiny things and stashing them, all lined up, on a beam in their attic. That is about the extent of her memory of her grandparents.

Diana heard from her sisters that their father's mother was the kindest woman around. It was not common in Germany to have big family-get-togethers in those days, but she would have all the families of her 9 children over for holiday dinners at their big farm, and never get tired of doting on her grandchildren. She would beg her parents to let her sisters and brothers stay overnight or a few days in summer, and she'd spoil them with things they never knew at home. She would let them sleep late in the morning and tiptoe around the house not to wake them. Her oldest sister was her favorite. When she was little she'd stay there more than at home while her parents had to work. It was a long way to her grandparents' house, at least a five-mile walk. Diana could not remember ever going there. Earlier her parents lived there for a while, because their father built a second story on their house, with a balcony that stretched all across the front of the house.

When her grandmother died, the estate was divided very unfairly among the children, as grandfather was already too old to realize it. They say that the son that did the least work was given the farm. One of the brothers went to America by boat. One of her father's brothers bought his own farm with his 4000.00 Deutsch Mark (DM) inheritance. Than the German inflation hit. When Diana's father received his 4000.00 DM, he stopped on his way home to buy a sack of flour. It cost 4000.00 DM. Lucky he was, because the next day there was no more flour to buy. The money was totally worthless, and there was nothing to buy - the German inflation after World War I.

Diana remembered stories of their neighbors' wheelbarrow full of 100.00 DM and 1000.00 DM bills – stacks of worthless money. The kids played with it.

This must have been the worst time for her parents. Work was sparse. Her sister remembered their father coming home after days of looking for work – trying to comfort their mother after giving her the bad news that he didn't find any.

It had to be one of the worst things for parents, not to be able to feed their hungry children.

Their landlord in Logan came to collect the rent - knowing that the children had not eaten for days, even though he had a stable full of animals and plenty of everything. There was no compassion. The rich exploited the poor. One time their father asked him if he needed the money more than his hungry children did - and the landlord said he did, sweeping the money off the table. Sometimes their father went out in the farmers' fields, too weak to swing the scythe, because he had not eaten for days. His wages were 50 pennies a day. For a liter milk or a pound of potatoes or flour a week they had to work for an entire season for a farmer. Her parents knew nothing but toil and hard labor, injustice and degradation and servitude under the most primitive conditions. It was a hopeless existence, an almost senseless fight for survival, no different than slavery.

Their father's brother later sold Diana's parents a piece of land, just enough to build a small house on. It cost 50 DM for 10 years and to barter both their labors on their farm for 7 years. Their mother nursed her sister-in-law's father for 3 years until he died, and nursed her after childbirth of her 8 children, kept house for them and took care of their children and animals. Her father helped build their house; he dug the well and laid the pipes of hollowed out trees under the street and half a mile down the hill from their own house to his brother's. He made all their families' shoes, wooden and leather for years. Both Diana's parents worked at their farm – for 7 years. All of this slave labor to have a little house of their own! When her father had committed himself to help someone else in an emergency for two days and could not work for his brother they cursed her parents and told them that they pissed on all their work. They did not speak for years, and they were not associating with them. Her aunt didn't like their kids around anyway; she'd had enough of her own. Diana only secretly walked to school with Erwin, her cousin.

Her parents felt used and bitter sometimes, but as good Christians they turned the other cheek… Not that they had any other choice.

Diana's oldest brothers and sisters were born in Logan. Her parents favored that village; they used to say that people were a little kinder there. They were more respected and felt more at home. After they built this house and moved to the farm-village of Hohen (all of five farms) ,they had a hard time getting accepted by those farmers. They were outsiders. If you were poor, you were judged and degraded and suppressed more.

This is why honor was so important. Diana understood later why they had to behave and not cause any trouble. Their parents could not afford anything that could be held against them. It was critical that they had a reputation of being honest, kind, decent, capable and charitable, that they had a good standing in the community. A job depended on it. They were so terribly dependent on people for even food to survive. It was important what people thought about them.

Her oldest brother Frank stole a roll of bread once when he was a small boy from a bakery/farm. He was so hungry and was looking at these rolls that he never had at home, as his friends coaxed him to just take one. When her father found out – and he most certainly did find out - he beat him to a pulp; then he told all his children that if they would steal anything ever again he would hack off their hands. They believed then and today that he meant every word.

This is how cruel times were then; they brought out the worst – or the best in people. Even uncles, brothers were relentlessly greedy, even envious if you survived. One day her mother broke down telling her brother in tears that they had no food for the children. He said he didn't care if they died of hunger. I guess you would have had to live in her parents' time to fully understand.

They were the poorest family around. Only because of her parents multifaceted talents and their persistent strive and enduring will did they survive. For seven years Diana's father couldn't find a job other than a day's work here and there for fifty pennies a day. He played in the town's band, and at the gatherings the guys would tease him because he couldn't afford to buy a beer.

During that time her father received a letter from someone he didn't know with 30 DM and a note: "To ease your poverty". He thought he had opened someone else's letter. He looked again; it was addressed to him. So he wrote to that man, even swallowed his pride, and thanked him, but asking how on earth he came to get his name. (Diana remembered the style of writing: "Most Honored Mr...." signed: "Respectfully and subordinately yours..."). That man was a doctor in Munich and would only say that he got his name "from a friend". Her father said later that this 30 DM had turned their life around.

Those were the time her parents lived in.

To them their father represented everything good, honest, just, fair and decent. He would give anyone the shirt off his back. He had a heart of gold. Though he tried to maintain a strict, authoritarian image, a little tenderness would occasionally show through. To Diana he was God's likelihood.

He had beautiful curly hair that turned totally white at an early age. He had the bluest eyes. They told everything. You could see to the bottom of his soul. When he was sad, you knew it – and they would smile and sparkle in some of the better times. The eyes are a dominant trait their family. Johnny, her grandson had her father's eyes – the little devil in them when he was up to something, couldn't hide it when he was sad or in trouble – and when he was happy, they would shine like a sunbeam.

With his children her father was very strict, sometimes more than he wanted to be, but he was strict as her mother wanted and needed him to be. She would wait for him to come home and she would tell on them. Diana feared that. She hated it. She hated the fact that she caused him to spank her more than the spanking itself. She knew he hated it even more than her. He was soft underneath his armor.

Elli and her brother Jo were inseparable. Everyone thought they were twins. Elli stayed very petite because she had rheumatoid arthritis, so her brother caught up with her quickly. When Elli started Kindergarten, her brother was so lost, he became ill. Their parents finally made an agreement with the school that he could sit with Elli if he behaved. He did. The trouble started when he had to go to Kindergarten again the next year. He was bored to death, and also very smart. He already could read and knew his math in first grade, and he had the memory of a genius. So he pulled straight "A"s in every subject, but the mischief his teachers endured lasted all the way through his eighth grade. They did not know what to do with him. His sister died a thousand deaths, feeling responsible for him and feeling sorry for him – because there was hardly a day he left school without swollen-up palms from the beatings with the "ruler" or the "whip" from his teachers. That was the traditional and allowed punishment for any transgression in school. After that he got a spanking at home for the obvious evidence of misbehavior on his hands. He didn't cry. Diana felt so sorry for him, and covered his butt whenever possible.

There were harsh times; there was no time for nonsense. There were limits. Obedience was a must for a child. It was never challenged. You didn't rebel. You didn't talk back. There were no

69

tantrums. Perhaps there were tears (and they were not allowed), but you obeyed. You didn't run away. It never entered their mind.

Diana remembered they were not allowed to talk during dinner. She always had trouble with this; she sometimes just couldn't be still. Her father would first look at them, and if they still said a word, he would slap them with his spoon on their mouth. Sometimes he would just hold the spoon up in the air, and they got the message. There was very little said. She has memories of another dreaded "spoon"; it was a spoon, but much too big to be used for cooking.

Her father had a tool-drawer under their kitchen table. This was hands-off. He could have a very bad temper if he found anything out of its place. A tool was a treasure in those times, a necessity of life.

Punishments were harsh and merciless – like the times they lived in – but they were structured and orderly. The children knew what to expect if they crossed the lines. They knew the lines. They were clear lines and a simple law of the "proper thing to do." They knew their place. There was cause and effect. They were not punished because their parents were in a bad mood, or drunk, or angry. It was to discipline them for what they knew they weren't allowed to do. They learned right from wrong quickly. Her parents needed to prepare them for what they knew was a harsh world. Yet for the children it seemed that there were just too many wrongs…

Diana only wished that they had been allowed to cry.

Her sister was 21 when she was slapped because her older brother, her chaperon, came home from a neighborhood dance alone… She wanted to stay for another half an hour… When she brought home her first boyfriend, the love of her life, her parents frowned on it. Diana was totally in awe of the two, they were obviously in love. In their time one didn't show affection in public, kiss or touch or hold hands. It was indecent. No one ever hugged. It was not customary in Germany. You didn't make a spectacle of yourself. The most cordial greetings was a handshake. There was not much room for that nonsense in their cold world. There was no huddling or cuddling in front of anyone, not even for kids. Babies would be hugged and cuddled until they could stand up and walk. Diana thought that this stuff was all a sin. She caught her sister and her boyfriend kissing and hugging several times. They were in love.

Their parents did not approve. He didn't have enough ethics, or job, or manners, or whatever. After he brought his mother over to meet her parents, it was over. She wore lipstick and nail polish and even smoked cigarettes. Maybe their parents had never seen a woman smoke. That was the end. Early the next morning her parents took it upon themselves to end their relationship. They told him it was over. Diana was there when they told him to leave. She felt sorry for him. She wanted to scream. She didn't. Neither did her sister…she secretly cried a lot.

Diana never understood this. She liked him a lot. They were good together. She never knew if her sister ever quite forgave their parents for this. She wouldn't blame her if she couldn't. However she ultimately respected her parents enough to let him go. It broke her heart. Later in live, both in their seventies, they met somewhere by accident, and her sister said, they still felt the attraction, they still believed that they had belonged together.

They all were sure that their parents wanted the best for them. Sometimes it was very hard to believe it. They feared for them and hoped for them for a better life, to protect them from all evil like every parent does. It was a different era. There were war times. The times had hardened them so that it must have been difficult to believe in trust in life and love anymore. Life was pure survival.

Her father. He was the provider. They counted on him. There was no job too hard or too dirty or demeaning for him, but there wasn't always work anywhere near their town. He would walk miles to get to a job. Diana can't imagine how bread got on the table sometimes during those hard times, and there were times it didn't, but it was never due to her father's lack of trying.

If one ever experienced hunger, one will not forget it for the rest of one's life no matter how plentiful your existence may be. They learned never to waste a thing. She could hear her father say, "Wer den Pfennig nicht ehrt, ist den Dollar nicht wert" – meaning "someone who does not value the penny is not worthy of the dollar".

She felt guilty all her life of being wasteful, and would pick up a penny in the street…

Diana's father built the house. It had a kitchen, two bedrooms, an attic and a small stable. It was not big, but it was all theirs, and it was home. He built it with his own hands, totally – with the help only of her mother and her oldest brother. Frank - at nine years of age - carried buckets of mortar as big as himself, they always said. Her father made the windows, doors and stairs, the roof and the fence, and every piece of furniture they had. He did the same for other people, to earn money for materials. Sometimes he even had time for a toy. He made her a doll bed she remembers well. It had a heart-shaped cutout at the headboard. The best carpenter couldn't have done it better. He built her several swings; she was very hard on them. When she was about thirteen he put together and fixed up an old bike for her from old pieces… This was the time when she grew wings, the first sense of freedom she experienced. She could fly… She could break out of her limited world…She could feel the wind in her face… It was a wonderful thing! She still has the wooden salt pot with the metal rim around it that he made for their kitchen. Her niece painted it lovingly with flowers. Diana treasured it. It was probably as old as she was. She could see her mother take a pinch of salt out of it. It always was the exact measure.

Her father was a contractor, a bricklayer, blacksmith, lumberjack, carpenter, shoemaker, farmer, tool-and-die-maker, butcher and baker and candlestick-maker…He was a genius. Not that he had all this education! He just worked at things until he figured them out. He was one of the first that could make leather shoes and boots anywhere in the area, and to perfection. They would call them the "Schuster" (shoemaker's) children. He was overwhelmed with orders. Everyone wanted some leather shoes. The leather was very expensive, and often people couldn't afford the shoes when they were done. He made them almost for nothing, and eventually he had to give it up.

He was a charitable man, her father. Charity and compassion were important values for her parents. Even in their worst poverty they managed to feel sorry for the "less fortunate"…Her mother believed that someday the kindness you extended to others would come back to you. However "true charity" was not to expect anything in return. Diana didn't see why they were fortunate, but her parent's generous thinking taught her regard for others, a sense of understanding. Her father often did not have the heart to charge for his work, because everyone was poor. People owed him forever, and sometimes he felt taken advantage of, because he had a family to feed, too. Diana remembered some of his turmoil.

She learned this extreme tolerance from him – to always be a nice person, to allow people to abuse her and make excuses for them…

You wonder why these honorable, charitable traits in their family produced so many Doctors, Nurses, Healthcare Professionals, Social workers, Martyrs, The commitment to others before one's self, even at their own expense and safety carried on. She herself was one of them, including her children, a grandchild, several nieces, their professions – healing, helping, giving - undervalued, underpaid.

Her father could sharpen everyone's saw, scythe or blade, better than anyone in town could. Later he worked for the forestry, building roads for the state. They had to make gravel, manually. Her father, with other men from their town, walked off before daybreak with hammer and chisel to split rocks into small pieces – for days, weeks, months. They laid the rocks into troughs of sand, so the splinters would not fly up. It was work. What a blessing! What her father must have suffered, trying so hard to provide for his family, yet forever at a loss. How demeaning for a proud man as her father to have to depend, to slave…

The work in the forest, especially the logging, was one of the hardest jobs for all the men in town. "Holzhauer" (lumberjack), became his long-term job. They had to cut down the huge trees with handsaws, then clear all the branches off them – in the freezing winters – and then load and chain the trees on huge sleds and guide the sleds down the mountains to the stream. In front of these huge loaded sleds they would stand, steering the sleds down steep slopes, for miles, with no brakes other than their feet. Then they would "swell" the stream and guide the logs down to the mill. Many men were killed, as their sled would run into a tree. It was very dangerous work. Perhaps that's why they sawed three crosses in the stumps of the trees they had felled "for the departed souls to find their way to the light".

Perhaps that tells that they were very much aware of their mortality, it certainly tells that they prayed a lot.

Her mother certainly prayed and worried much in those days. She would look out the window every evening, waiting for him to show up at a clearing several miles down the hill. Their cat Peter seemed to know when he was coming. He would sit on the front steps just about the right time every day – and they knew then that her father was right around the corner.

Later, when the State started building roads through the "National Forest", her father was commissioned for the job. He knew engineering principles without ever going to college, and always ended up a foreman. He could not stand incompetence and was a perfectionist himself. He was a man of strong convictions and not afraid to stand up for the right thing. His motto was "Tue recht und scheue niemand", meaning Do the right thing and fear no one.

Diana wished I could have followed his advice more in her life.

Hardly anyone would ever challenge him, because he stood his ground. He was very strong willed. Later he was a Union steward, speaking out for fair and equitable treatment for the workers. He was always fighting for the underdog, a trait Diana inherited from him. He certainly was not a politician, her father. He had his own ethics.

All Diana's life she was drawn to defend and justify and feel sorry for anyone in trouble, always fighting for others, not herself.

There was money to be made now. Work was a blessing. People were thankful for work. They worked with pride. No one ever turned down a job. They really believed that "Wer nicht arbeitet, soll auch nicht essen", meaning: one that doesn't work should not eat either. Diana remembered the heels were always gone from her father's boots. They were his brakes, while steering the sleds down the slopes. She often helped him take his boots off when he came home, that was an honor – and they would soak his frozen feet. She wanted to blame the boots… After he came home from work, he would lie down and rest a while on the "Ofenbank" (the wooden bench behind the stove); it was warm there. That was his favorite place. The men would take a thermos with hot coffee along to work. The sandwich they ate was usually frozen. No wonder her father had ulcers. He never complained.

One day he came home with a handkerchief wrapped around his hand. He reluctantly let her mother take it off, only to look, not to touch. He had cut off his thumb, through the bone; it barely hung on by a flap of skin. He had glued it back on with sap from the trees. It would stay that way, with a handkerchief wrapped up again until it healed. Back to work the next day. No work, no pay. The thumb healed back on. No nonsense. They were rugged people. Times had hardened and toughened them beyond belief. They didn't have a doctor in town anyway. You had to go several villages away to find one. No hospitals, either. Babies were delivered at home by a neighbor, or possibly by a midwife, if they could find one. Newborn babies sometimes died. Mothers died during childbirth.

Her brother told her that he remembered when their aunt down the street had her babies, eight of them in all. The first thing they would do is dunk the newborn in the ice-cold water in the trough outside, summer or winter. "If it is fit to live, it'll live", they'd say. These babies lived. It was all about survival. Weak babies would become a burden to the family.

This was life. People were tough. Old people or sick people lived out their lives with little intervention from doctors or anyone else, often with much pain and suffering. There were lots of home remedies and salves, hot water bottles... and something like Epsom salt to soak, Diana remembers. Aspirin was a rare commodity, but they had Peppermint-, Chamomile-, Fennel tea, and all kinds of herb teas from plants and roots. She remembered her mother making her Fennel tea for stomach cramps; she must have had colic.

They would get paid for collecting a particular plant or root. Diana remembered collecting the roots of a yellow flower exactly like the St John's Wort that was later being studied and thought to be a better remedy than Prozac – supposedly without side effects. They would put drops, Belladonna and extracts of all kinds, on a sugar cube – for some ailments, such an anxiety, heart-or stomach pains. She knew her mother taking some of that occasionally. Her father never did. He never complained. He didn't drink much or smoke much, even when he was young.

Diana never really heard their parents fight. There were a few words, and her father's was always the last. At least her mother let him believe that. She was very diplomatic. Diana never remembered him being unkind to her. He truly cherished her, and she liked his attention just fine. Diana was sure that they had their trials and tribulations, but there was true compassion, total devotion. She never thought that their love for each other ever wavered, though she never saw them hug or kiss. Their private lives were sacred.

They had a strong Family unit. Her father was without question the head of the family.

Even as adults none of her sisters or brothers or she would have ever talked back to him. Even later in their lives they would whisper - just reliving some experiences – taking great care not to sound disrespectful toward their parents.

They always felt safe and secure as long as her father was home. She remembered how lost they were during the war when the SS drove all their fathers out of town, arrested them, or shot them. When he disappeared they didn't know if he was alive or dead. To lose their father was inconceivable.

One Christmas her father cut pieces of wood off old tree stumps in the forest, and with this free wood he made all sizes of wooden shoes, at least 20 pairs of them. He walked without a coat in the freezing winter from village to village trying to sell those shoes. Christmas Eve came; he had been gone for three days. The Christmas lights were lit at the neighbors. At their house there was no Christmas without her father. On Christmas morning her father came home, half frozen, some shoes still in his bag – but he was home. Now it was Christmas. He even brought some flour, and apples, and nuts…

One time some men, including her father, were commissioned to work at the forestry of a faraway town near Munich. She remembered her mother crying her eyes out when he left. After two months he came home and he brought an entire outfit for her mother: a dress, hat, shoes and all. She pranced around the house, modeling them for days. He brought flour and bread and apples and pears, and a wooden jumping jack for Diana.

Her father played in a band. He could play every band instrument, but he was the best at the clarinet. She recently came across a picture of their band in a book, and she could not believe how much her grown-up son resembled him.

They found out in the later years of her father's life, that his stomach was so scarred from all the ulcers that he had all his life that the doctors couldn't operate when one of the ulcers turned cancerous. He was hospitalized and died there, of a side effect, a stroke. The family said he waited for Diana to arrive from the US, he then died in her arms within the hour.

After all of their children had left home, her parents sold their home; the house her father built with his own hands. With the proceeds they helped her oldest sister build a home for her six children. Then they helped her oldest brother build his home. He also was struggling with a family of five children. Next came her sister Elli and family, and then her brother Frank with his family of six children.

Diana's parents couldn't change the way they had lived all their lives, no matter how much their children tried to help when the times got better. They were not used to having, and afraid of losing. They couldn't comprehend better times – times without hunger and war, hardship and despair. They looked cautiously at the "better times" - always afraid that they might end tomorrow…They wouldn't part from the 40-year-old oven or table or their old clothes, and they ate as in the times of hunger…"Just wait 'til the depression comes again", her mother used to say. They would not afford themselves any modern luxuries, such as a toaster or a washing machine, or God forbid a television set, and all presents they stored away like they did during the war…They had no wants or wishes, they didn't think they deserved… Diana's parents were chained to the past. This was how her parents spent their "retirement": Moving from place to place - depending on which one of the children was building at the time. They helped all of them build their houses, except Diana. She knew it burned a hole in their heart that they could never help her. She hoped that they knew that they gave her the best they could have ever given her – the strength and fortitude and tenacity to survive despite anything. She learned from them to persevere. Surely they knew she was the most stubborn of all and the most driven, and that nothing would keep her down for long… by God's grace.

Sometimes her parents walked into her life later in her life with a presence so strong that she had to stop and listen – and she would still feel her mother's eyes on her…

She made the difference…with a dab of jelly…

She was born in the year 1901. Diana's mother was the most beautiful girl in town, not only according to her father. She was true blue. She was kind and charitable, and always gave more than she had. She was always helping someone, or nursing someone that was ill, as if she did not have enough to do at home. Her brown hair was waist-long. She wore it in a neat, tight braid like a crown around her head every day. Diana could not remember her any other way. Her hair never turned very gray. She was beautiful inside and out into her seventies. Her name was Carol; she was the youngest of nine children of the Stoch family. Her parents were from Bohemia.

Diana's parents were married for 51 years. Only a year ago she learned from her sister Elli a big secret about their parents that she was never told. Apparently her mother's parents did not acknowledge her relationship with her father. When she would not give him up, they disinherited her and threw her out. Yet later, her sister said – grandmother would visit them, and she would bring some candy or rolls for the kids. She always said that she wanted to die at her mother's, and one day she came over, and did, for real, she died in her arms.

Her father's parents were not much help either; they had 9 children of their own. Diana's parents had not married yet when her mother became pregnant with her oldest sister. In their time that was – to say the least – socially unacceptable. Already poor, they became outcasts and shunned everywhere. Diana never knew her grandparents. They lived a village away.

Her parents found a small shed to live in next to a blacksmith's shop. When her mother became pregnant with her second child, they were married. Needless to say, life was very difficult for them. Work was hard to find. Yet sometimes her parents talked about these days fondly. There was no border between Bavaria and Bohemia yet, and they were free to go to Winterberg, a City in Bohemia that was quite beautiful. With some friends they would pile into a wagon, pulled by oxen. It took several days for the 60-mile trip. Perhaps this was where her mother had seen all the pretty things she had in her head. She always had a million ideas. Diana could never figure out where her mother learned of things so different from all that was around them. Her parents never complained about how difficult their early marriage was. They moved around a lot to villages wherever they could find work and afford the rent. Hardship and poverty followed them everywhere. Eventually her father built a small house and had three more children.

Diana's mother was strong and determined. Her resilience made an enormous difference in her own life. She transformed their bleak and often grim world into a bearable environment. She made the difference with a dab of jelly on their everyday pudding, a pad of butter on the farina, a pretty button or tassel on an old sweater, a warm brick in an ice-cold bed…She could work miracles. She could make something out of nothing. She made everything they had: their bedding, featherbeds, their mattresses filled with straw, their curtains, schoolbags, all their clothing. She could knit and darn and weave and spin and sew. She knitted stockings and mittens, the hardest thing for Diana to learn, sweaters and tights, and everything without a pattern. When a sweater couldn't be fixed anymore or they had outgrown it, she would rip open the yarn and knit a new one of it. She would cut up two pieces of old clothing, and make a beautiful tailored new one of it. Many evenings she remembered winding yarn with her mother; there was a trick to rolling it into a perfect ball. She taught her string games with old yarn, and making things out of every snip of fabric.

Diana could not have been more than 5 years old when her mother let her sew on their old "Singer" sewing machine. She had to stand; her foot couldn't reach the foot pedal well. This was not an electric machine; you had to pump the foot pedal to make it run. Her mother would show her how to make little dolls and doll cloths. They were sticks tied together crosswise with a cotton ball for a head, and covered with a piece of fabric, then tied at the waist. She made dozens of them.

They didn't have many toys, and the few she remembered were handmade. Most kids' favorite toy was a teddy bear. She knew they couldn't afford such a thing. She never craved what she couldn't have. The first thing she would by for her kids, Diana vowed, would be a teddy bear. She did.

Every doll she ever had was handmade, except one. She was a gift from her uncle's girlfriend who worked for a doll factory in northern Germany. Diana never understood why she gave that doll to her. She was not used to getting gifts. Perhaps she was the only little girl around. This doll was beautiful, stood two feet tall and had socks and shoes and real hair. She had a porcelain face and hands. Her father made a bed for her. She was the most precious toy Diana ever had. Only one day she broke, and her heart broke… She never liked any dolls since.

She always thought her mother made the beautiful colored clown for her when she was about six years old. She could never remember what became of that clown. She thought she must have lost it, or something traumatic happened to her at that time that explained why she disliked clowns forever after. She knew that ever since she had a distinct apprehension and disdain for clowns and she never felt a need to replace it. Perhaps there was no room for a funny clown in her life; maybe it was too much irony…Somehow a clown didn't fit into her world. Now her sister told her that her brother Jo brought that clown to her when he came home for a visit from the Tool-and-Dye-school he attended at fourteen. It must have been the last time she saw her brother…That explained it. Maybe she blamed that clown for her brother's disappearance shortly after.

Her mother was the most resourceful person that ever lived, Diana could swear to this. As poor as they were, and believe it, they were poor, there was always a hand crocheted or embroidered tablecloth on the table. You'd never guess that their drapes were made of bed sheets; the elaborate embroidery made them look like a million dollars. They had embroidered pillowcases, aprons, handkerchiefs and doilies, lots of doilies. Diana often wondered what could have possibly motivated her mother to even think of trivial things such as embroidering during those hard times. She worked so hard to improve things, to make life better…

Later in her life Diana understood her, because during the most unlikely times of her own life she did the same thing. What she did was important, it was something that justified her existence, proved that she was valuable and needed. She would never give up if she could make something better. She herself was able to create, pull up, to hope and wish for the better life, the beautiful, the constant.

She was industrious, her mother. She would get everyone out of bed every morning at daybreak for no other reason than not to be lazy. Diana herself knew no different. All her life she remembered her mother saying: "Don't leave for tomorrow what you can do today". Even though they were poor she took pride in the fact that their clothes were always clean though mended with many patches at times. She would even darn and mend their friends or neighbors kid's clothes. No sock had a hole; they learned to darn at an early age. Poverty was no excuse to be sloppy. The one pair of leather shoes they eventually had were to be shined meticulously. That wasn't easy, because they would be either wet like a sponge, or hard as a rock after they were hung to dry over the stove. German people have a thing with shoes. You can never polish them enough. It is an old custom: You judge a person by his shoes. Diana's older brother used to make her polish their shoes, and after she thought she was done, upon inspection, she had to do them over at least once or twice more.

Perhaps that's why Diana was never particularly fond of shoes. She kind of enjoyed wearing dirty gym shoes out of defiance, she guesses. She would never wear boots. They might be the best, the most stylish, beaded, studded, carved western boots –She had no use for boots.

Clean and orderly! Their windows always sparkled; their wood floor was scrubbed on hands and knees (regardless of the slivers) every day. There was order in the house in the worst of times. It was a constant, something they could count on. It held them together. It kept them sane.

There was a reason why Diana liked order, especially during messy times of her life. She needed order to hold her together. She needed things in place, files up to date. It was not a matter of control as much as a basic sense of self-preservation, of staying afloat. Not unlike her mother. Diana learned to be punctual as a little child. The rule was: "Wer nicht kommt zur rechten Zeit, muss warten was uebrig bleibt." That was: Whoever was late, got what was left. In her case it was supper once, and there wasn't much left...

They were poor. Nothing much grew in their rocky ground. The summers were very short, and the winters too long and severe. People totally had to depend on the land, what they could grow and harvest in the short season, and the Grace of God. Sometimes her parents rented a small piece of land from a farmer to plant potatoes or just for hay for their cow, and they planted something on every square inch. They had to work for the little piece of land a whole season.

As long as she could remember back, before and during the war- and post-war times her father and mother would do any job, they would work for anything. They worked for farmers for just milk or flour or potatoes. Her sisters and brothers worked at age twelve or thirteen for farmers as well, not for pay, but for supper, because there was not enough food at home. Fourteen was the age to leave home and work, at least for the poor. Her brothers were rented to farmers to work in the fields, clean and milk animals, tend the herds and clean stables. Her sisters were maids, nannies, cooks and slaves for big households. Don't think that these young children were spared any work, or given any consideration. Once when her mother was sick, she sent her oldest son instead to mow the grass in the fields with a scythe. He knew the work well, but the farmer – mad because her mother didn't come – swung the scythe under her son's feet all day, threatening to cut off his feet. Some of these big farmers were very mean.

There was always food on the table, sometimes not much. There were never any leftovers, and nothing was ever wasted. The bread was kept in a locked drawer. Sometimes her mother reflected on it later, that she did not know where the next meal would come from. Sometimes they were hungry, but mother said, they should be ashamed to complain. It was a sacrilege to "want more" They should be grateful for what they had. Diana could taste some foods half of her life, the blueberry potato strudel, the "dampfnudels" (sweetbread dumplings) with vanilla sauce, dipping bread into buttermilk, the "rahmsuppe" (cream-egg-soup)... She cooked some of her mother's recipe all her life, and a tomato reminded her for years of the first one she tasted as a teenager.

Her mother was a great cook. She would cook up something, soups made from flour or farina, or potatoes. She could make more potato dishes than anyone could imagine: Potato stew, -pie, -rolls, -soups, -potato and flour crumbs in lard, -dumplings, -pancakes, etc... Of course, hunger was the best cook. The things they ate were unbelievable! Diana had to check with her sister, because she thought that maybe she had imagined them, but it was just as she remembered. They picked the leaves of the "Brennessel" (Poison Ivy plant) and other weeds, such as the "Sourampfer", a real juicy weed that even "made the cows happy" they used to say. Mother would make soup of these, or dip them in pancake batter and fry them. They were good. They were food. The "Sourampfer" they would eat in the fields, as well as poppy seeds. They had no idea about effects. No one ever talked about allergies either. Perhaps these weeds served as antidotes, or maybe people just took allergies in stride like everything else.

They never knew fish. They were totally foreign to them. There were no rivers anywhere near. Meat was a rare occasion. When a pig or a cow was slaughtered somewhere in the neighborhood, which happened usually at Christmas time, the neighbors would get together and help. They would eat the "blood soup" that Diana couldn't stand the thought of, and make sausages. Their father would work for them for some meat. It was a feast for them like Thanksgiving. Most of the time, a good size pork chop or a steak that size would be divided into four or five servings. She relished a selfish thought that some day when she grew up she would eat one of those all by herself.

Later they even had a butcher in town, but the meat was still scarce, and to was the money. For some time they had a few chickens, but even if they could survive the long and harsh winters, the foxes would raid the chicken coup at night, and they'd find the feather trail into the woods in the morning. She would sometimes find one of their neighbor's hen's eggs in the woods behind their house. Mother said it wasn't theirs to keep. The sparse fruit trees that grew in the area were sour apple- and pear trees and cherry trees. Oh, the cherry trees! Berries grew wild, raspberries, blueberries, strawberries, blackberries and currants! Her mother would make wine from berries of all kinds. She loved berries. You could pick blueberries and sell them for a few cents a basket, and they would pick berries all day in the season. Sometimes they were even allowed to use the grownups' "berry comb", which accomplished a lot more, but they had to pick out the leaves and bad berries later. For weeks they were covered with blueberry stains from head to toe. Diana learned to apply a tourniquet at that time, when a snake bit one of the kids.

Some people were shot and killed during blueberry picking near the Czechoslovakian border, they said, by the Russians, but no one really knew for sure. What did they know about one war zone vs. the other? The Russians were on one side, the SS on the other, it was all the same for a child: a dangerous world. They would look over the border at the deserted village with burned down houses, ruins and lifeless streets, grass growing on the roofs. They were used to war. It was everywhere. However, after a few kidnappings and shootings they were not allowed to go blueberry picking in the high forest anymore, and they understood not to test their limits. No wonder people just rather stayed put and conformed to the rules even after the war was long over, and stayed sheltered and afraid to venture out of that town.

They had a very small garden, just a ten by twelve strip along the side of their house. In spring they grew cabbage and carrots, rhubarb, lettuce, herbs and spices, and a few rows of potatoes, of course. Her mother had at least one green thumb, just not enough ground to plant in. However they planted flower seeds in every square inch around their house and in their window boxes, which her father made, Pansies, Carnations, Forget-me-not's and Cosmos every year.

Diana favored these flowers forever.

Tomatoes, oranges or bananas and many other fruits and vegetables she did not know or taste until sometimes in her teenage years.

Once they had a pig, and then a goat – for milk, and a sheep, which served as wool for their socks and sweaters, but the baby sheep they kept. They raised it with a baby bottle. She was Diana's favorite pet, and she taught it quite a few tricks. Later they had a cow, their most prized possession ever. Only she needed more food than they had. They fed her every scrap of anything resembling food, potato peels, garden scraps, dirty dishwater…They walked that cow on a rope like a dog every day – to let her graze on the side of the street on common land until she was full.

They had to be very careful about the "common land".

One day a neighbor caught the cow taking a mouthful of grass from under the fence. She ran down and kicked the cow in the belly, and the cow lost her calf. Diana remembered her sister coming home crying with the moaning cow. Her parents were very angry and unforgiving about that incident, and Diana was never to go over to their house again to play with their girls Annerl and Marille, – the only girls around. She understood, because the cow was survival. What her parents didn't know was that the neighbor's cherry trees, not as much the girls, were such a temptation for her that after a while she would risk the consequences and sneak over there again to climb the cherry trees…

They had very little land for growing grass for their cow. For the feed for winter, her mother cut grass with a scythe in the high forest miles away. Even that they had to pay for. She carried it home, uphill, stacked up on her back in a big basket. Diana was sure that basket weighed more than she did, it was three-times her size. As a child she felt the weight of her load, and she thought her mother carried "the world on her shoulders". Then they would lay the grass out to dry in back of their house, and tied the hay in bundles for winter. She'd go as often as necessary, until the shed was full. Diana walked with her all the miles. She remembered her struggling up the last hill sometimes, setting the load down on a tree stump one more time to rest.

She would help her slip the strap of the basket off her shoulders. Her mother hated to stop to rest, because it was so hard to get back up. Diana remembered feeling helpless and horrified when she saw blood streaming down her legs to her shoes from the hemorrhages she used to have.

After the war they had a General store, and they could buy some things they had never seen before, that is if they had money. Diana remembered her mother sneaking a few pennies in her hand to buy some rock candy, and they shared the other tiny candies, they were smaller than mini skittles. She thought her mother liked them as much as she did. It felt like a big secret, like they were "partners –in- crime" squandering money. This she remembered as one of the kindest moments with her mother.

On her way home from school she often had to buy a loaf of bread from a farmer. They had an outdoor oven as big as a house. It was built for baking bread. People would jokingly threaten to throw bad children in that oven. (Hansel and Gretel) That oven was huge and scary enough to make one behave. You were never sure they wouldn't do that. These were big, round loaves of bread, and they smelled so good from a mile away. They were always supposed to make the "sign of the cross" on the bread before it could be cut or eaten, to thank the Lord. They didn't' take this lightly. Bread was life. They knew what hunger felt like. Many times Diana would pick away at an end where the loaves had stuck together. She was always hungry. That was a big temptation. She always got in trouble when she came home. She did it again.

One of the "big" little things she will forever thank her mother for is this: They were sleeping in the unfinished attic – under the bare roof – and it would snow on their beds and freeze the spot they breathed on the featherbed. She dreaded to go to bed. The frozen wood stairs even would crack and cringe, as they would walk up to the attic. They tried to be very brave. Sometimes, on the coldest days, her mother would make it all better: She would warm up a brick or a steel cover of a frying pan in the oven, and she'd put it in their "Strohsack" (straw-sack-bed) under the featherbed. It warmed up the bed deliciously. Diana could feel the great pleasure of sliding into the warmed-up bed many times in her life.

Her mother was an artist in every sense of the word. She really had talent. She could draw anything, name it, in a flash. So did her sister, she could be a cartoonist. Diana had no idea where her mother learned calligraphy. She must have remembered, or copied it from old books. Diana learned the basic scripts from her mother. Talk about good taste, she had a sense of balance and colors. Something would bother her about a picture; she'd hang it somewhere else. It didn't fit.

She had original ideas. Diana remembered when she painted the walls in their kitchen. She made her own cardboard stencils that created beautiful designs on the walls, and a border at the ceiling like flower pedals hanging down. No one had seen anything like it. She vividly remembered making paper roses and tulips… paper airplanes and pop-up advent calendars. She had a million ideas, her mother. They made their own watercolors with some powder, and they always had enough to paint, if not on paper, on rocks, trees, and everything she could get her hands on. Paintbrushes were rare treasures. Her father knew how to make them of hair from a horse's tail. Diana was one of very few kids that had a paintbrush. She loved to paint and draw; she remembered some favorites: mountains, winter scenes, forests, Christmas trees, chimney sweepers for "good luck" in the New Year, spring scenes and Easter bunnies. Everyone thought she was good at it.

Her mother also loved to sing, not that there was much to sing about. In her days you had to make your own music. Radios or record players were a real novelty; no one she knew had one of those. Somehow, there was always a harmonica, accordion, zither, guitar, flute, drum, horn, clarinet around somewhere, and someone always played one of them. The only instrument Diana hated, were the drums. They reminded her of the war. The SS had marched to their beat.

Later in her life she learned that her mother loved to dance and laugh and enjoy fun when she was young. Diana did not remember her that way. She could not remember many humors during her childhood with the exception of Luggai. He was really a cousin of hers, but so much older that she always considered him an uncle. Her mother was the youngest of nine children, his mother one of the oldest. He was a genuine clown and he loved to entertain with his thousand faces and a wit and talent that could put the best comedians and impressionists to shame.

When Diana was about twelve years old, her parents got a zither from someone. They actually paid for her to get lessons. She had to walk or ski four miles to the instructor who was the pastor in Logan, every two weeks. Within a few months she could play quite well, and her brothers would accompany her with their guitars when they came home. Perhaps that would make them come home more often. Her parents seemed to enjoy it, too. She played with her brothers at a couple of weddings and small gatherings. They were proud of her, she could tell without them ever telling her. Both her parents encouraged her to play music. They said that if you had a talent, it was a responsibility. You should not waste a God-given gift. That somewhat inhibited her.

She would have rather just enjoyed it without obligation.

Diana wrote a couple of songs when she was thirteen. One was about one of the prettiest lakes in Germany, the "Koenig-see". Ask her husband today, he'll agree, they visited that lake. The other was about her home, the beautiful Bavarian Forest. She heard later that someone had recorded her songs, and one was played on the radio. They still remembered her songs at home.

Her mother was also very sensitive and perceptive. Clairvoyant…you would call it today. Diana swears that she had not five, but nine senses. There weren't many external stimuli, people were deprived of so much, so they developed internal senses and instincts beyond the norm – like blind people. Her mother knew of things ahead of time. She saw things in a dream that would come true the next day. Her father was playing with the band when they were young, and she had a dream that someone was stabbed at the "Wirtshaus" where they were playing the following night. She begged her father not to go, but he had to. She thought it was he that was stabbed; she saw the whole thing, blood running to the door… That night her father's cousin was stabbed and died there

And where was Diana's brother, Jo? Everyone was afraid to ask anymore. He had just disappeared. He had signed up for a tool-and-dye apprenticeship in Pilzen, Chechoslovakia, then occupied by the Germans. That's the last thing anyone knew of him. There was no communication, and every one of those boys was believed to be dead. It was at the height of the war. No one knew anything, except their mother. She knew he was alive because she heard him screaming in her nightmares, and calling "mother" over and over. She knew that something terrible had happened. Once she saw soldiers – in her dream – throwing him in the ocean. He could not swim. She saw them driving a motorboat over his back – and him struggling to keep from drowning. She saw blood squirting up and heard him scream. Later they learned that these events were true to the letter. Seven years later, Diana's brother came home. On Mother's Day 1949, her brother came home, and nothing was ever the same. Her brother was one of the few survivors. He didn't talk about his experiences for years. No one dare pressed. Much later he would tell bits and pieces.

The school in Pilzen had been bombed and set on fire, the boys chased on the roof...the few survivors were transported to the northern war front, finally captured by the Russians, and transported to Siberia. Once Diana heard him telling their parents some gruesome details, bits and pieces she never forgot. The boys "thrown into the freight train like animals, jammed in like luggage, the dead bodies dumped off along the way." He told of the excrements and the foul smell of dead bodies above and beneath them. He told how they were stripped of all dignity, enduring desperate thirst and hunger. Not many survived the concentration camps very long due to Siberian elements, ferociously cold winters with no food other than grass, worms, bugs, snow and dirt.

No one could measure the effects of emotional damage, starvation, frozen hands and feet. They would take their toll later. He was the only survivor, they said, that had teeth …

But he was home. He made their entire town believe in miracles again. He left as a young boy, and came back as an adult. He said he might as well been dead. Diana's brother said – had he not come from the extremely poor conditions and tough times at home, he would have never survived Siberia. He was always fine if anyone asked him. A Master in tool and die, he had 6 children. He had endured many surgeries including valve replacements, an amputation, kidney dialysis, and yet if asked, he was always "fine". Diana never forgot him telling her much later in life, that he was proud of her. She felt very humbled. Coming from him, she considered this the biggest compliment she ever got from her family. As for her mother, no one questioned her intuitions ever again.

She was scary, her mother. Diana remembered someone once having an Ouija board. When her mother's turn came to try...her hands flew across the board and gave a message that scared everyone, and came true to the letter. It was a message regarding her uncle who was missing in the war; the word came that he was dead. He was. It bothered her mother so much; she would never touch anything like a Ouija board again.

One could never get away with lying to their mother. She would tell by their eyes. Forget it. Diana hated her disapproval. She would look right through her. She often felt when something would happen to her, or other events in town, ahead of time. She wasn't looking for it. She hated it. She called it a curse. This stuff scared Diana stiff.

She remembered this dreadful thing about mirrors. There were no mirrors in any common places. One would think they still lived in the 14th century when mirrors were exclusive for nobility. The women in their town would hide a small mirror in a private place. Theirs was only about three by five...the size of an index card. It was the only mirror in their house. Her father was the only one using it to shave. She couldn't remember her mother ever looking in the mirror. It hung so high up on the wall that Diana couldn't see it anyway. In any case she was warned: "Vanity is evil. If you look in the mirror, the devil will look out at you." She feared the devil, she feared God. She had heard this so often, that she believed it. The few times that she climbed on a chair to look in that mirror she was really just checking if she was growing "horns", she knew that to be a sign of allegiance to the devil. Throughout her childhood, especially at times when she had tested her limits, she would imagine growing those "horns", that were an inevitable punishment for her defiant nature. She was actually uncomfortable with mirrors half of her life.

Diana didn't like herself a lot anyway. She was never told that she was pretty. She would have loved to hear it even if it wasn't true. The spaces between her front teeth and her too big nose always made her feel very self-conscious. Her long hair she had to forever wear in two plain braids. It was never very pretty or shiny, considering that it was washed with soap. They didn't have shampoos and conditioners, lotions or perfumes. Trying to improve one's looks would have been considered vanity. She always felt guilty for having those vain thoughts. At last she resigned herself to the fact that there were some things she couldn't change about herself, like how her hair forever after parted in the middle, no matter how hard she tried to make it part on the side. There was nothing to do about it. You stayed the way God created you. The image of one's self was totally unimportant. People didn't believe in any cosmetics. Her mother never wore any lipstick or makeup. Her skin was pure and flawless all her life. Her secret: Never wash your face with soap. Diana followed that advice, and her mother made a believer out of her. In any case, it was considered a sin to change ones image. People did not believe in choices. Choice was power. Power was bad. It was not for them. They were poor, and they were supposed to be humble and subordinate.

Diana was about eleven years old when her aunt took ill. She had TB and was bedridden at home. Her mother volunteered to take care of her, because her family was not able to. They would walk to her house a couple of miles away every day or two, and her mother would bathe her and feed her, and make her comfortable for the day. She was getting worse, and her mother said Good-bye to her as they left that day. She asked her several times to send for her when she needed her.

The next morning they were sitting at the kitchen table, her mother and herself, looking at pictures in their big bible. They would read together, especially when it was too cold to go to church. The bible was the only book she remembered other than their schoolbooks, and the storybook of "The Brothers Grimm". That was it. They had no library. Anyway, as they were reading the bible, someone was coming. They both looked up and wondered who it might be. They heard the footsteps coming up the stairs to their fore house, a small shed in front of their house. They heard the house door open, they heard someone stomp off the snow, walk three to four steps to their kitchen door, wipe the feet and – no one came in. Her mother got up and opened the door. No one was there. There was snow on the mat. She closed the door and said: "Did you hear someone coming?" Diana said, "Of course. Where is he"? Mother sat down and nodded as though she knew something. A few minutes later, there was someone coming up the stairs. You could hear the frozen stairs crunch, shaking off the snow, opening the door, a few steps later wiping the feet again…and then… silence. Her mother turned white in the face. She didn't get up right away. Diana had goose bumps all over. They just looked at each other, and she finally got up and opened the door. No one was there. Just more snow on the mat Diana sat like she was nailed to the chair. Her mother slowly came back and said quietly, "She is gone".

They fiercely tried to concentrate on the readings. When this happened again some ten to fifteen minutes later, Diana thought they would have both jumped out of their skin, if the door had not opened. It did. Freddy, her cousin, stood there, he was about her age. Before he could say a word, her mother said, "I know... she is gone". She took Freddy in and sat him down, and then she asked him if he was here before? He said, "No, she just died a few minutes ago. I ran all the way here". Believe what you want, Diana was there. She had goose bumps every time she thought about it for a long time.

They were Catholic. They went to church at least on Sundays, rain or shine, winter or summer, unless the roads were totally impassable. This was much her mother's doing. People clung to their faith. She never understood it as a child. It sure didn't give her any joy or comfort. All the women wore dark clothing forever, and covered their heads with a big black scarf. She remembered the Sunday service. It was morbid. The church was dark, the Mass was said in Latin, and the sermon was about the impending wrath of God - or a meet with the devil's evil forces... It was about repenting and penance and punishment Diana never knew what for. She just never remembered it being about joy or "Good News". Had it not been for the Pastor coming over to the house to anoint the dying, the hope and promise of a spot in heaven after this miserable life, and just the desperateness of their situations, their tortured minds – people might not have gone to church every Sunday. It was a capital sin not to go to church, the consequence condemnation and hell in the afterlife. That fear prompted most people to go to confession on a regular basis. Their mother saw to it that her family did. Yet Diana never really believed that things could ever be forgiven.

Everyone went to church. The men would be gathered outside the church in a huge congregation, which promptly after the service moved over to a nearby "Bierstube". The women and children attended the mass. Her mother would be checking with her father if he actually was inside the church and knew what the sermon had been about. Their pastor was very angry with the men outside, but was never able to change their habit. One Sunday, he yelled from the pulpit to open the back door of the church so the "men folk" outside could hear him as well. Then he raised his voice more than usual.

There was prayer, a cross in the corner of their kitchen, the "Herrgott's Eck". It was always adorned with a few flowers. Before dinner they said grace. Everyone stood and faced the cross. There was an "Our Father" for someone that was sick or in trouble, or had died, for people that had died in the war – I don't know which war. They said a prayer for the "poor souls in purgatory" and for a "peaceful hour of death". That always made Diana cringe. She had nightmares about it; she was always scared of her parents dying. Death was very real to them; it was in their face all the time. By the door hung the little Holy-water-cup, and you sprinkled yourself as you left the house. On special occasions, at every "Right of passage" such as leaving to get married, or for a safe journey, or a dangerous job the parents would bless each other, or them, and make the sign of the cross on their forehead with Holy water.

There was a rosary; her mother would hang on to it for dear life sometimes. Diana wondered how many thousands of rosaries she said! Half the town would meet every week of the month of May for the rosary prayer service in a little chapel. Mother made them attend, come rain or shine. She always thought she could keep all of them safe with her prayers. Diana wondered where she would have been without them. How she could talk about being "peaceful in the center of your soul" - in her world, she will never know.

When she goes to sleep at night sometimes - Diana hears her mother say: "Never let the sun set on your anger." This was the secret, she said.

Diana was glad that her mother taught her to talk to God, even though she feared him and she never knew him as the loving God, but at best as the refuge and Savior in all their desperate situations. The faith was there, and the hope, only the love of God was missing. However, despite all the changes in her life and the churches' views of some issues she herself had never forgotten how to pray.

Her mother died a peaceful death – 5 months after her father – in 1973.

When Diana visited Germany years later, they all visited the Cemetery, where their parents were laid to rest many years ago. They said a prayer, and sprinkled Holy water on the grave. One would not believe the abundance of fresh flowers and plants on the graves there. People take care of the cemetery with a devotion that is foreign to us in the U.S.A. There were fresh flowers all year, and the pine trees are decorated for Christmas. It would be a disgrace to the family to neglect that duty. It was a matter of pride and honor, and respect for the dead. In the USA, this immigrant and transient country, many people have no choice but to bury their loved ones in their hearts only.

Diana realized that she never called her mother and father "Mom" and "Dad", none of them did. There always was a "respectful distance" between parents and children. That was more important in those times than a "loving closeness". Diana could not remember any of them hugging their parents, or each other. They must have done so as little children.

It took for Diana to move across oceans to bridge that distance between them. She broke the ice. When she came home from the U.S.A. she would hug everyone. She had become accustomed to it in the States, and she liked it. She was no longer inhibited to express her joy of seeing her family and relatives. Her sincere exuberance went far beyond the customary "handshake". She knew they all welcomed it as well, because they are not so reluctant to show their feelings anymore today. Now everyone in her family is used to hugging each other at least on occasion. She could tell that the German reserve and rigidity had softened when she watched her nieces and nephews interact with their children. What a joy! It's about time! It's about breaking the chains – it's about being free…

Did their parents love them – even though they never told them? Diana thought their life certainly was the proof. When she was grown up with children of her own Diana's parents once told her, that they wished they had done a lot of things differently.

Diana knew that they had very few choices about their way of life. She told them that they did their best.

V

ALL   SHE   HELD SACRED

What was a convent? To explain a convent – especially a convent of the 1950"s in Germany - Diana admitted she finally consulted the dictionary after being at a loss for finding the right words. Later it reminded Diana too much of a cult.

There were several related entries in the dictionary. "The state of life of the members of a religious order...a community of persons devoted to religious life under a superior, a body/society of persons living by common consent under the same religious moral and social regulation… a practice of sacred rites and observances…"

Its members lived in seclusion from the outside world, other than a very few nuns with very limited social contact, such as teachers, nurses, etc., and contact only for that specific purpose. Religious practices included prayer meetings, Silence, and other rituals, vows and commitments for "spiritual growth". This way of life was considered a "Marriage to Christ and the Church", and was based on the main commandment, the cornerstone of the Order: total subservience to a superior. On the outside it all looked so admirable. Under the veil of this religious blanket, sanctioned by the strongest influence of the times, the Church, it was acceptable to everyone.

When one becomes part of this life, one closes the door to the outside world. One gives up family and friends and all contact with them. One gives up everything that is dear to one, and leaves the world behind. As Jesus said to the Apostles: "Leave everything and follow me" .Diana did in simple faith.

Ten years she spent in a life she had trouble putting into words. Or was it just too complex or overwhelming and painful to remember?

When Diana was thirteen and had finished Grammar school, a new "Middle School" had opened in Frey that kids from their area had to attend. There was no high school in the European school system. The new middle school was finally an interim opportunity for further education and trades. Frey was fourteen miles away, and the only way to get there was by bus. Diana's parents finally figured out after she had lost twenty some pounds in a few weeks that she was either allergic to diesel fumes or motion sick. She vomited day and night. So they bunked her at a farmer's house in Frey for a couple of months, so she could walk to school and finish the semester. She didn't know the people. She was on her own. They fed her and she had a bed to sleep in. She remembered feeling displaced, lonely, lost and abandoned. She would have never admitted this to anyone. Something broke in her at that time. Her parents considered it a good short-term solution. The farmer's son was a teacher, and she had such a crush on him.

The end of the semester came and Diana didn't' think that her parents knew what to do with her. There weren't many choices.

A missionary priest was filling in for their sick pastor, who had emotional problems ever since the SS arrived. He wasn't at their parish for very long. He said that he has to move around a lot. Diana remembered their old pastor well, because he used to twist a bunch of your hair right at their temple, as he would walk by their desk at school. It hurt like hell. He beat the kids with sticks and whips over the head or wherever. He could do this because he was the Pastor. That new missionary priest was much nicer and greatly respected in town. He thought she was smart, he said. He would frequently select her for songs and readings in church. Her mother was flattered that he talked to her in Diana's behalf. He recommended a one-year girl- school with room and board in Passau, in which he could get her enrolled. She would not only have a school curriculum, but also learn all the household duties: knitting, sewing and etiquette, etc., a must for any girl. This was certainly impressive to her mother.

Diana didn't know who convinced whom, it sure was not hard on her part to decide. She was packing a bag with a few clothes and personals shortly after. She was actually supposed to bring 6 pairs of underwear, stockings, shoes, and a few other things they didn't have. She was taught that there was no shame in being poor, but never forgot the embarrassment and agony she felt when the few homemade, washable menstrual pads were never enough to last her through her period, and she was too ashamed to ask anyone for more. She remembered never having the right size bra and wearing the only one she owned for years, mended and extended with various "alterations" of her own. These private things were unmentionable.

For the first time in Diana's life she hated being poor.

Somehow they didn't have to pay tuition or room and board, which they didn't have anyway. They were very grateful to this priest who would look out for Diana for some years.

When her parents dropped her off at the convent school she didn't realize that it was "Good-bye" for many years. Her mother told her that the superior of the convent promised her to "keep an eye on her."

Diana was open to everything good, and anxious to learn. She was never so happy in her entire life. She loved every day and every minute there. They were thirty girls – it was heaven. Some girls were homesick. Not her. She did not want to go back home. She did the best in school. She made friends.

She lived in the "good-girl" complex, opposite the "bad-girl" complex. She never did find out what these "delinquent" girls had done. She always wondered. No one ever said. They were never given any contact with these girls. All she knew was that they were different, they would yell obscenities across to them; they had no privileges and none of them ever left. It seemed like a jail. She never knew it really was a juvenile detention center. She had no idea why she was sent over there to supervise the 30some girls during their lunch break sometimes. Was it supposed to scare her? These girls liked her just fine. Was she one of them? She was conflicted with this. They were bad girls. Diana didn't want to be one of them. It scared her. She considered herself very lucky that she was safe from the evil things they must have encountered out there in this big bad world. She was going to be a good girl.

That year was too short; it was over in a flash. What next?

To go back home just wasn't an option. What would she do there? Someone said that there was a way to stay. She could enter the convent as a candidate. That couldn't hurt. She told everyone that she wanted to stay. No one asked her why. She was so grateful that they accepted her, and she didn't have to go home. She was going to be the best nun ever. If servitude was her life, as she knew life to be, she might as well serve God. That must be honorable.

The convent was a New World for Diana.

Her parents gave their permission rather easily. She had no desire to go back home. She was fourteen years old. Her brother and sisters told her later that they understood that she had to leave home, and were not surprised that she entered the convent, even though they objected to it. There weren't too many options. It was the time to leave home. They all had to leave home at fourteen, sometimes earlier.

Later her mother confessed to her that it had been the answer to her prayers... When she became pregnant with her, nine years after their fourth child, and hardly able to make ends meet and survive – she prayed that "God would take that child", because they couldn't handle any more...

Deep in her soul Diana found this very hurtful. She always wondered what exactly her mother meant by that. She never quite forgave her for it, but she never told her that. Only much later Diana understood.

In their culture and religion women had no choice, they were not allowed any form of birth control, abortion - God forbid - not even abstinence. A woman was married to bear children – however many she could have or feed.

Diana's mother considered her entering a convent a blessing, the answer to her prayers, God's will – hoping that this was her "calling". Believe her, so did Diana. She thought it was a good thing to take that burden off her shoulders.

As it turned out, her mother especially was very proud of her for "choosing this respectable, holy, safe way of life". She really believed she was very blessed. Who knows what trouble Diana would have gotten into otherwise! This would keep her on the straight and narrow.

Her parents were in their fifties, and worried about her growing up. They were already so tired, so beaten and worn out. The wars and their endless struggles had left their marks on them. There was still no work or industry, or educational opportunities anywhere near their town, and she guessed they wanted better for her than marry a farmer, and work for a farmer. A long time later they told her that they thought she had a lot of talents. So did everyone else, her teachers, the priests, and the nuns.

Diana, on the other hand – taught to be humble and never acknowledge any compliments – didn't believe she deserved any attention for her talents.

At fourteen she thought she should carry the world on her shoulder, she was going to be very responsible. She would behave well, be a good girl, and stay at that convent forever. She counted her blessings every day. Everyone liked her, and that alone was something she had never experienced. She wanted to be good so badly, that she met with everyone's approval. She radiated so much youthful idealism, and her heart was in everything she did. She loved the idea of everything pure and good and holy. It was safe and respectable and honorable; even her parents would have to agree. This life couldn't be any harder or poorer, any more hopeless or demeaning than theirs had been.

Perhaps she felt becoming a nun would make her more worthy and less afraid of the wrath of God. Perhaps there in the convent she would be one of his favorite children. You see, considering the religious temperament of their time and her childhood, they only knew the fear of God and his punishment, equal to the fear of the devil, condemnation and hell. Everything was a sin. There was no room for being human. Being a nun, and being so perfect, would have to eventually wash away all the fears in her tortured little soul.

Diana was totally serious and devoted herself with heart and soul to these high ideals, commitments and vows. She offered herself to God. She entrusted all her cares to God. The nuns used a picture of her as the "happy, idealistic young nun" in one of their advertisement campaigns for attracting new candidates. She would never leave the convent. She even conquered the outrageous rule of the convent: Absolute silence. They were only allowed to talk in a group for a designated hour a day. Her… who couldn't keep her mouth shut during dinner.

She thought it not such a big deal to make a commitment to the three major vows either: Poverty…She had had enough experience in that, she thought. Chastity…who needed sex? That was sinful. Obedience… she was taught all her life.

When she took her first one-year vow and received her veil, her hair was to be cut short, very short. This was a major ceremony. She actually had long, beautiful hair, they said. This ritual was symbolic of giving up one's pride and vanity. She remembered saying that her hair didn't mean anything to her, and gave it up willingly. By that time she had no worth or pride. The issue of her hair did not matter. All contact with the outside world was severely discouraged. Only for the ceremony of "taking the veil" a supervised visit of family was allowed. Her proud parents and her reluctant sister came to witness her giving up her birth name, her identity, the last connection to them, and the old her. She told them that she was happy. Everything else seemed insignificant. She remembered that she had to ask her parents to buy her black shoes. She said they didn't have the money, but no one believed that they were that poor…The other nun's parents were often bringing gifts and money to the convent, they said.

Diana learned to conform to the controlled environment of the convent, to a behavior that was suitable for a nun… "Cast down your eyes…pull in your lips… never cross your legs… never show emotions." She followed every rule. She went where she was sent, and did what she was told. They worked in the laundry, the kitchen, the yard; they painted and cleaned, and prayed…their day was scheduled to the minute. There was no idle time. They were committed to humble and simple duties before they could hope to be called to heroic ones. Diana only recognized now her talents and achievements, at the time she was just doing her duty, her best. She went to school and she worked nights on artwork, stationery, cards and pictures for all the religious occasions for the entire convent. She conducted a choir with thirty nuns, composed and wrote most of the music for church and all celebrations, and copied the music thirty times (there were no copy machines). She could write music faster than a letter. She played the church organ, read and wrote songs and poetry, and her heart was full of joy.

For a couple of years she was sent to a teachers college, another institution of a different religious fraternity. She took a bike alongside the river for about 5 miles, the river that was there every day the same, some stability, in any weather. The river became her friend. She never looked left or right. In those days a nun on a bike was a sight. She didn't mind being ridiculed. She was proud to be a nun, she thought she was worth something. She was proper and loyal. She had a liverwurst sandwich every day and an apple. Often she felt tired and overwhelmed. Underneath it all the feelings of shame and isolation were haunting her, so she repressed them.

It was at that college where she became somewhat conflicted. The nuns at this institution would sometimes talk to her regarding her priorities and her commitment to her convent (vs theirs) but she always rejected their concerns. Fondly of that time she recalls a sister Gertrud, her Piano teacher, she was so kind to her that Diana was very tempted to trust her. She recognized Diana's artistic and musical talents and encouraged her to pursue them. She loved to write but her subjects were dark and much like herself, conflicted. Diana remembered a student, a girl named Maria Poplau she played a concert with, Mozarts "Das Veilchen" (the pansie). Maria did the vocals, she played the Piano. Diana botched it. She was so nervous. They both loved writing music. She really liked Maria. She also kept and treasured Maria's original hand-written "Ave Maria", she sang it once in a while. Diana wished that she had been allowed to be her friend.

Diana was told that she was very good at that school. Of course she was not accustomed to handle a compliment. She almost resisted the feeling of pride, remembering her childhood warnings "not to get a big head." However it felt good. She further studied piano besides the school curriculum. She liked all her other activities better than school work. Her grades were not her priority. She accepted the fact that she was "different" because she was the only nun in the class. She was not allowed to mix with other students or have any friends, or join after-school activities, just like during all her childhood years. She convinced herself that it didn't matter, that she didn't care. She was committed to her cause.

Why then – at that time - did she use her lunchbreak to run down the hill, through the entire city, across the Danube bridge and up the 100s of steps to the chapel of "Maria Hilf", where it was said miracles happen? What exactly was she praying for so desperately every step up? Did she feel trapped? Did she try to escape at least in her mind? Diana never allowed herself to reflect on her experiences from that time. That would not have been proper.

At her convent no one hardly spoke to her, no one counseled her, and when the second year was up, she was not considered suitable or promising for anything they had hoped for. School was cancelled. She was set aside. Diana felt very isolated and depressed. She met all her religious obligations, prayer meetings, etc. just fine, and got along with everyone. Often she had assignments 'til late at night, and the alarm rang at 5:00 A.M. Mass was at 6:00 o'clock, and she remembered struggling so hard to stay awake. It seemed that she was always tired and exhausted. For many years she secretly wished that she could sleep late just one day, sleep until she wasn't tired anymore...There was such emphasis on spirituality that one's physical well-being was unimportant. Their examples were Saints that had courageously suffered pain and torture without complaint. How could one complain about fatigue or headaches? Diana never saw a doctor, never had a physical examination in her life.

Food was bland and sparse, but even if there was enough she never took any pleasure in eating anything in particular, respectful of the plain fact that food was for survival, and grateful that hopefully she'd never go hungry again. She distinctly remembered even later in her life choking down baked potatoes with nothing but dry cottage cheese every Friday. She couldn't recall what a bathtub or shower looked like in this convent, nor whether she took a bath or a shower during the 10 years there. Either was done as a necessary evil, she was sure. To take pleasure or delight or joy in "earthly things" was not appropriate in a convent.

Except for Christmas and Easter and a few religious Holy Days, they were not allowed to write home, or anywhere else, and the mail was censured. Even after everyone else had accepted this, Diana's sisters would write to her once in a while, and her parents did as well. She couldn't write back. She couldn't keep any reminders of her past life, no childhood pictures or other things. Telephone calls were out of the question. No one had a phone at home anyway. Diana realized that her parents had relinquished all rights and claims to her. They were not allowed any vacations or visitors or other contact with the "outside world".

In Diana's case there were a couple of exceptions shortly after she entered the convent. One was her brother Frank. He didn't take "No" for an answer. After he had found out that her parents had given their permission for her to join the convent, he showed up with his motorcycle and demanded to see her. He told her then in no uncertain terms to get her stuff and get on the bike, and he was going to take her home. She was so embarrassed. It took her a while to assure him and explain to him that she was not going home. He just couldn't believe that she would do this. He had hopes and plans for her, someone told her later, and he was really disappointed. Did he miss his little sister? Diana wished he had told her that, it might have helped.

Another exception to the visiting Rule was the Missionary Priest that brought her there; he would come to their convent a couple of times a year. It required special permission for her from Mother Superior to see him and he would speak a few words of encouragement to her. Once, when she was troubled with something he reminded her of the song: "This cannot shake a seaman…" She hummed that song for days, it reminded her to stand tall and to be brave. Her superior promptly told her that this was not suitable. Somehow she thought of that priest as someone in her court, just in case she ever needed an anchor in a storm…After all, he brought her there. She did not understand why his visits were frowned on. Maybe her superiors didn't want any interference. After a few years he didn't come anymore. Diana always wondered if he had his own secrets as he seemed uncomfortable with her adoration and respect for his priestly status. Diana wrote to him at Christmas and Easter, and said exactly what she was supposed to say, what a good nun would say…"Reverend Father… may the blessed Holy Child give you peace…"

Diana tried not to forget everyone's birthday, even though they were not allowed to write. Her mother thanked God that she was so protected from all evil. Little did she know!

In the ten years she spent in this convent she was allowed to come home once on a brief vacation. She visited a guy she went to grade school with, just a mile into the town. His aspiration supposedly was to become a priest, her mother said. Kindred spirits, Diana thought. Yes, she realized that all eyes were on her, since no one had ever seen a nun before. She overstayed a little, and it was almost dark by the time she walked home. That was the time her father followed her home with his belt dangling in his hand for all the world to see, all of the two miles back to home. Diana couldn't describe the embarrassment she felt. Was he afraid that she might become too comfortable at home? Perhaps she would stray from the convent? Diana felt that she was grown up, and it was clear to her that she could not live at home anymore, that she did not belong…

Somewhere along the way she had grown up, she thought. Somewhere along the way she surely lost some of her youthful idealism and enthusiasm. She learned that people were people everywhere. She saw more of the human dark sides than she wanted to believe. She would have thought a convent to be the most unlikely place for these less honorable human qualities and behaviors such as jealousy, unfairness, dishonesty, gossip just to list a few. These were contrary to the values she was taught during her childhood. There at the convent these behaviors were neatly disguised and covered up under the cloth of religious pretenses. Sometimes they were hard to recognize as bad and evil, but her gut instincts were never wrong before. It was confusing. She became somewhat disillusioned along the way.

It bothered Diana that she was always looked at as "too young" and "too inexperienced" and "having no idea of what the big, bad world was like". She wanted to know what other nuns knew; she wanted to know just what experiences she had missed by entering the convent so young, as they always implied. Once, a new candidate walked around in a trance for a year at least – everyone had to be extra nice to her. Later Diana heard that she had been raped, and that's why she was in the convent. She wondered if she was supposed to have had a reason to be a nun, and if everyone did. She respected and looked up to the other nuns as though they were Saints already. Then again, some of the nuns were certainly no saints, including some of the superiors – misusing their authority, passing their whims and wishes and often unfair decisions off as "God's will". Obedience meant giving up one's will entirely, and without question accepting a superior's word as Gods word. It scared her later to remember these things. This entire concept could be severely misused and abused. She had seen it in action. It was like a cult. Of course, their convent at that time was probably very old fashioned and certainly too severely regimented for a young child. It was not likely what you would find in later times, and was not meant to discredit all congregations, religious or otherwise. (You see how she would make excuses...) The experience was for her unhealthy and crippling, it only accentuated her already strict and authoritarian upbringing. It left her severely intimidated by authority, and with feelings of inadequacy and unworthiness and fear of punishment for most of her life.

She saw more of real human fallacies than she could understand and digest: nuns having affairs with a priest, their pastor being so drunk that he was staggering at the altar, internal politics that weren't "holy" anymore. There was money spent on things and people that did not befit a convent. She took the vow of poverty very serious. She saw things behind the scenes that she could not justify with her beliefs and integrity. She learned that people were not what they seemed to be. Her hopes for doing great things and making a big difference in anything dwindled.

Yet she tried to keep her focus on her ideals. She went everywhere she was assigned to be, and did what she was supposed to do. She held her convent in the highest regards. She closed her eyes. She tried.

Early in her convent years she learned to change her nature. She was always chastised for being "immature", the child she was, and not too lighthearted by nature anyway – but craving to be happy. It was out of character for a nun to laugh or be silly or funny. It was not suitable for a nun to show these emotions. She was expected to be serene and composed and serious at all times. She never wanted to appear taking things lightly. She thought she had to prove that she took everything very much to heart. That's when she consciously stopped laughing. She learned to curb that urge, suppress her natural feelings and conform. She was a serious child anyway, never had much reason to laugh, but she always envied people that could whole-heartedly laugh. She wanted to laugh like them. She even tried to change her laugh to a deeper, more adult one, but it just wasn't suitable.

Diana later regretted that she couldn't create a more carefree, lighthearted environment later for her children, as much as she wanted to and thought it important. She had to make a conscious effort to laugh, like she had to "free" her soul. She considered the ability to laugh such a precious and healthy attribute, but it needed to be allowed to burst out the joy and merriment - freely and spontaneously. Diana thought of laughter as "water springing over the rocks in a brook", freely, uninhibited, naturally. She admitted that this quality wasn't hers, and her soul was not free. She so admired it in other people.

At about nineteen, she was assigned to revive an inner city Kindergarten in a northern German city. At that time, she had been working in the nursing home with extremely ill and dying people. She liked working there, though it wasn't hard to change from the dying to the children. She did her best at both. She could help. It was her calling, God's will. Naturally she loved the children with her whole heart, but she wasn't supposed to allow herself to get involved and attached, according to the disciplines of the convent. She wasn't supposed to love one job more than the other, or love anything with "earthly" feelings. She gave up the human emotions; they were to be dead.

She revived the Daycare/Kindergarten. She doubled the attendance of children, hired enough help, even her own nieces, a decision she questioned later. She felt that they were deserted, left all on their own, since she was not allowed communication with them. She bought and organized play centers with the new Montessori-toys, held meetings and conferences with all of the parents, which was unheard of before, and certainly not encouraged. The parents looked up to her - to her surprise, her at nineteen… She would have loved to do more. She was always warned not to become too friendly with these outside people. It bothered her that a nun was considered above a "woman of the world", a mother, a nurse that was not a nun, or any ordinary "unholy" people. Diana felt nothing but admiration and compassion for these mothers' roles in life. Many of them were on welfare, some were abused, the children abused. Some of these mothers were Saints…something didn't fit. The nuns thought that their "calling" had put them above the rest. Diana was not sure now that this was a wrong interpretation of the concept of the Order. They were supposed to be humble. She had been taught more humility and modesty in the simple sanctuary of her home during her childhood. She thought a convent to be a strange place to learn about arrogance and hypocrisy. She despised these things for the rest of her life.

There were huge gaps in her development from childhood to adolescent to adulthood. They would have to be bridged later in her life. Leaving her family home as a child of fourteen, brought into an institutional environment of a mass community of adults that had chosen this way of life – she was certainly misplaced. Time seemed to stand still for her. Yesterday was gone and tomorrow was far away. She lived for the moment oblivious to a course or plan. No one was interested in her personally, how she felt, who she was, not even herself. She thought she could just skip the process of growing up. There was no normal healthy, age-appropriate environment that would have allowed human feelings to develop as they are supposed to during the growing-up period of a child. It was a sin to be human. Diana had learned that as a child. Now even more so - in the convent - they were to kill everything unholy, which was about all-inclusive. One followed the rules and religious obligations, trying not to step out of line or call attention to oneself - being humble, selfless, dead to the world, unanimous among the shadows of the others. One gave up one's identity. One gave up all freedom, the freedom to want, to wish, to choose. There was no room to be human. Who wanted to be human anyway? One was going after Sainthood…

In this culture Diana learned to become someone other than herself. She gave up laughter, and she had long forgotten how to cry. She never nurtured the child in her inner soul, nor did anyone else. She gave up her desires, her goals and ambitions. She was never allowed to become her own person. She never grew up. From then on she was busy trying to become someone she was supposed to be. She tried to fit into the mold. She built a fort around her feelings, to protect them – and no one could penetrate her armor.

Yet deep down in her soul she was hurting. She was a fake. This was not her, the innocent, open, genuine, sincere child that had come to this convent. She felt deceitful and miserable. Her parents had instilled strong values in her – most importantly to be "true to herself". She knew she was a disgrace to her parents, a disgrace to herself. The person she had become wasn't her. How her mother despised "a wolf in sheep's clothing"! Diana despised herself. Sometimes she remembered praying that God put her feet on the ground, and give her back reality and clarity to see where she went wrong. Things were wrong. Yet she had to fit into the mold. Something broke in her at that time. She allowed her soul to be imprisoned.

Diana would never forget the weekly "purging meetings". They were a certain religious practice once a week. All the nuns would kneel on the floor before the superior - and humble themselves by confessing their innermost faults and any impure thoughts and transgressions, to lay them bare before the entire congregation. This was to teach them humility! Diana used to feel as low as it would go. She would make up things to say, because she couldn't come up with enough faults. She hated herself. She guessed this was not about absolution. She couldn't even forgive herself for whatever there was to forgive.

It was admirable for them to put themselves down and think of themselves as unworthy. The greatest Saints considered themselves as most unworthy. So she worked on erasing every thread of self-worth and self-esteem…this strategy tied very well into her childhood culture of subservience. How on earth she ever recovered some sense of self -worth and value after all that was beyond her later. It was no wonder that she had to struggle for the rest of her life with low self-esteem, lacking every belief and confidence that she could ever achieve excellence in anything.

Time went on… She prayed and sang her heart out. She loved the celebrations and the Holy Days; she created plays for the children, and choir productions for their religious community. She could never do enough; no one ever said it was enough; no one was ever pleased. She was not to seek praise or satisfaction or reward. She busied herself with all the important and holy things and tried to find God with desperation…yet she couldn't find herself anymore…

She used to have this dream – repeatedly – running through fields to find a certain spot near a brook where the most beautiful flowers grew. She'd be so thrilled and pick a whole bunch in a hurry. For some reason she could never cross that brook, and it always seemed like she'd done something forbidden, and she had to rush back. She had the same dream again and again, but there were fewer flowers every time, and at the end there weren't any. She would go back there several times in her dream to check again, and couldn't find any more flowers.

Sometimes Diana thought about sitting in the cherry tree as a child… looking down on a chaotic world… as detached from it then as she was now… seeing her life revolve around her, below her, through her, without being part of it.

Sometimes she would sleep with her window open at night, even if it was freezing outside – just to see the sky and feel the fresh air, desperately longing and trying to find her place in this world. It was an unrealistic world.

What happened to her free spirit?

In her early twenties - someone took an interest in her and enrolled her in the new nursing program at another location. Diana didn't realize what a blessing that was in disguise – because those three years were the ones that opened her eyes to a lot of things she had not been exposed to yet. They would determine the direction of the rest of her life, even turn out to be the lifeline when she was about to sink. Her nurses training was hard, but a valuable experience. She couldn't wait to graduate. During these three years she had a Superior that made her life a living hell. She would belittle and humiliate her in front of everyone, point her out as a bad example, criticize her work and put down every move she made. She'd assign her a project, and when she was finished, destroy it in a way that destroyed her, too. Music she selected for the choir she would call "kitschig", meaning child's play, or not "classical" enough. Diana's voice would crack during a solo, because her throat closed up when she kept staring at her. Her piano plays "lacked class". It left her with a complex and severe inhibition that haunted her for the rest of her life. She remembered falling over her own feet, walking into the chapel, because that superior would belittle the way she walked.

Diana thought she had buried these hurtful things, but even many years later most are easy to retrieve. Some of them she forced her memory to delete permanently, some that she didn't want to think about ever again...

She remembered when this Superior told the entire congregation that she was "too good" to do any manual labor now that she went to school. Diana washed convent walls for days to prove that she was wrong. More than ever now she wanted to be humble, the least, the lowliest, the "least worthy" of all. That was being a good nun. When she was finished late at night she stood in front of the closed kitchen door just like she did as a little kid in front of the locked bread drawer, hungry and devastated. The only thing she could find was a jar of strawberry jam; she ate the whole thing.

Even later she found the thought of strawberry jam reprehensible.

This superior influenced her nursing instructors, her assignments and grades. Later she heard that she told her instructor, who was a nun as well, to arrange for her to fail the finals and not allow her to graduate. She told Diana herself that she got by "by the skin of her nose". Yet all the three years she had good grades and was considered an excellent nurse by the doctors and patients. She doubted for a long time if she could be a good nurse, a good anything for that matter…

This Superior always treated her different than all the others. She would even have other nun's spy on her. She made it her sole mission to interrogate and ridicule and shame her continuously, above and beyond a reason that she could possibly attribute to her "Godly" authority; and when Diana tried to please her in the worst way, she'd ignore her. It was confusing. She told herself that she wasn't there to be liked; she wasn't supposed to seek approval. She realized that that person was determined to destroy everything in her. She would justify this torture by telling her it was for her own good, her "purging" before she could take her "final vows" to stay in the convent forever. She needed to be tried and tested, she would say. The strange thing was that none of the other nuns were tried and tested…

Later in her life Diana would call it emotional abuse.

Then it seemed just "too human" for this Godly authority figure. Somehow she displayed envy of Diana's meager musical talents, since that superior had been the only one to lead the choir and play the organ and piano before Diana came along. She couldn't understand it or at that time consider it a motive for the things she did, because that superior was so much better than Diana ever hoped to be. She admired her talents. She wanted to look up to her and respect her. She needed a mentor. So she fought like hell to do everything she expected, and couldn't understand why she couldn't do anything right, and why she kept punishing her unjustly. She only looked for fault and inadequacy in herself and never even considered any "human" motives on her part. She often thought about that superior's motives later, but at the time she was her superior, Diana was not allowed to question them. She had taken a vow of obedience. Besides, she was brought up to respect authority, and her religion taught her not to judge, not to hate... and with blinders on she wasn't able to see the bad in people, certainly not expecting such things in a convent.

In retrospect she clearly saw that her superior's motives were no other than petty jealousy and fear of her potential to be something better than what she had in mind for her. Someone told her later that she considered her a threat. Would she someday excel in something, and prove her wrong? Diana could not have cared less about her own talents. She had no goals other than to be a good nun. Any other aspirations and ambitions she had already left behind. She surely communicated that. A blind man could have seen that she had "died to the world" and all the "worldly" pleasures. At some point she finally had to admit that this Superior simply hated her. If she could have, she would have stashed her away on some forsaken island. In fact she shipped her off to Berlin for a typewriter course for six months. The supervisor there was like a Saint, and treated Diana the same as all the other nuns. When she came back the difference was the more noticeable, and it dawned on her that it wasn't her fault. Yet she kept trying to do her best.

These three years finally broke Diana's spirit, and at some point she hit bottom. She didn't recognize God in this anymore. She wasn't herself anymore, she wasn't the person that God had created. She wasn't connected to God anymore. There were too many questions deep down in her soul.

In retrospect she saw that that superior did her a favor. It showed her the way.

The most important vow she remembered was "to be true to yourself". That's what her parents would say. In the end her self-preservation took over. What was her mission in life? What was her calling? She was plagued by questions. She could not reconcile things she saw and experienced with her own ideals and beliefs and expectations. She wanted to do heroic things. She had wanted to be a Missionary. How she envied another non for being selected to go to Kenya, Africa! She had a Superior, a mentor that groomed and pushed her. Was it all about politics? Diana knew in her heart that she too had the potential for something greater. She had wanted to be where it mattered, she wanted sacrifice; she wanted fire… If she stayed in the convent, and even after she gave up all her wants, her own ideals and goals, and died to herself, too – was she just doomed to a life without heroism, without purpose? What was the purpose of all this? Yes, they had learned that one was supposed to carry ones cross; that was supposed to be heroism. What cross?

Diana had no idea what they were going to do with her. No one ever talked to her. She felt stranded. Obviously she was not considered suitable or capable of doing "big things". She couldn't even do little things right. What was her mission? Was she just meant to exist, lifeless, at the mercy of a deranged Superior who was just all too human in determining her fate? What was her cross? Was it that she had not yet given up her will, and was fighting subordination? Was she still a rebel? Was it that she wanted to be free to make choices about her life? Diana was encumbered with so many commitments that she could not see a "window", she could not imagine being "free" to do anything. Her spirit was fighting for survival.

One thing she knew for sure: she needed to have purpose. She wanted to help, teach, heal, grow – not be stifled, not be burdened with so much human baggage weighing her down so that

122

she was barely functioning. She wanted air –she wanted her life to be more…She wished someone would have answered all her questions, but they stayed just that: questions – for many months.

Diana became ill with a terrible cough, bronchitis, fever and whatever. For more than a week she stayed in this small attic room - barely able to get up, for weeks she didn't get to see a doctor. Medical care was arranged by her superiors, and only if they found it necessary. She was property of the convent. She had never felt so alone and abandoned in her life. She realized that no one there cared about her, or what would happen to her. It made her remember that she had a family, and she missed her parents, her family. Finally a doctor was summoned. She was hospitalized and told that she had TB. That was enough to scare everyone. Diana's family wasn't told that she was ill. No one from the convent came to see her for two weeks, and she thought if she died, no one would miss her, there just would be one less nun in the world. She was being transferred to a TB sanitarium. She couldn't tell you how terrified she was. The day before her transfer the doctors took the last X-rays, and they were clear. The doctors were puzzled. She believed in miracles like never before. She was then diagnosed with Psittacosis (Parrot's disease), a lung infection that showed on the x-ray the same snowy picture as TB. She had apparently contracted this from a Parakeet on the children's floor at their hospital. She was treated accordingly. Had she been sent to this sanitarium she would have surely contacted TB there, she thought – not that anyone cared...

Looking back - she supposed that they were afraid at the convent that she would infect everyone with TB anyway (just in case the doctors made another mistake), and she didn't think they wanted her back. She knew there were some negotiations going on to move her to another facility.

At that time of emotional and physical turmoil and confusion – the Superior of another branch of the order came to "rescue her" and took her back with her to the Kindergarten and Nursing Home where she had previously worked. Diana's final vows were weeks away. She was extremely "run down" in every respect, and she was grateful that this superior allowed her to sleep late sometimes and physically recover. She treated her so warmly, and made small allowances for her that she wasn't used to. She was honored and puzzled that she was this interested in her, especially after her experience at the previous location, where she couldn't do anything right. She thought she meant to be kind to her, approaching her in such a "motherly" way. Lord knows she needed her mother. Diana was very naïve and unaware that there was more than one sexual orientation. It took her a while to even think of it as a sexual approach. Yet she wasn't used to being hugged and caressed by anyone. All she knew was that it did not feel normal to her. It was improper. It was uninvited. It was unwanted. This was a convent; every nun had taken a vow of chastity. No one ever physically touched. No one had ever been this nice to her. Perhaps the superior knew that she was hurting, maybe she felt her turmoil, and this was her way of trying to help her?

That nun was in her fifties and was her superior in the convent. After a while this superior would find numerous occasions to be alone with her. She chose her frequently as her companion. One day she pulled her head back to rest on her large breasts, and she stroked her face and kissed her. Diana froze. She was paralyzed and confused. Her superior knew it. There were other occasions where she would come to her room, touch her or even stroke her breasts or her thighs… No one ever told Diana what a lesbian was. No one even acknowledged that there was such a thing, and if there was, it was certainly irredeemably sinful. Sexuality was not discussed in her nurses training. She had never had sexual feelings or contact with anyone. All sexuality was sinful according to her upbringing and religion. This was not normal, it must be even worse .It must be a sin. Diana felt that she was really perverted and bad, and had arrived at the lowest point in her life. She wished again that she could just die. Was this her fault? Had she invited this somehow by being so needy? She felt guilty that she had allowed this to happen, that perhaps she had shown some vulnerability, a need for attention, or even invited this behavior by her passiveness or ignorance. She didn't have too many choices, because she was too intimidated to say "no", and she was never asked.

Because she was her superior, Diana respected her authority. She couldn't handle any more confusion or describe how troubled she was. It was like an emotional hurricane. She felt violated and exploited by this authority, that very pillar that had dominated and carried the structure of her life had crumbled. She felt like she had given up all her power. She had done that in good faith. She felt like an innocent, unsuspecting, vulnerable five-year-old child that was raped. She went to confessions to try to cleanse her tortured conscience of all the miserable guilt and shame she assumed. At last she buried it deep in her soul, and never allowed herself to dig it up for many years.

Diana knew that she had to get out of this situation. She had to leave, yet she had no idea where to go. It was the last straw. The fire had gone out. There was no joy in just praying and singing anymore. All the values she held sacred from childhood on were uprooted and destroyed. All her high ideals, her faith in the "good and holy", her good intentions – or illusions – of convent life were shattered. They seemed unrealistic, untruthful. She had lost all trust and dignity.

Diana's life had come to an impasse. There was no back, there was only forward. Here she was now - fighting for her identity, fighting for her honor, her pride, her will, her soul, and the basic human need and right to survive that she was born with. These very things she had given up in the convent. It took all she had. She had almost forgotten how to fight. She had to change direction to keep alive whatever little she had left. She guessed that she was not quite dead to the world. Diana was willing to accept that perhaps after all her hard work and sincere intentions she wasn't a good nun after all.

A child - in an adult world...There were so many gaps in her level of maturity. There were so many things she didn't know. She had not bought her own clothes or shoes, or food, she knew nothing about money, housing, budget, medical care, getting around, driving a car...This religious blanket - their convent – had smothered her and shielded her from the real world. She had no idea what the real world even was. Was she strong enough to face this outside world she had left behind and denounced so long ago, ten years ago? Ten years is a long time, a crucial time, especially if they are the formative years of a child.

Could she face the humiliation of having failed at what she had set out to do? Could she deal with the disappointment of her parents? Had she disgraced and dishonored them by having failed, by leaving the status they were so proud of? Could she deal with the ridicule of some disappointed and disillusioned people that she surely would encounter for some time to come? Deal with any of it?

Diana didn't even want to get up in the morning. She was unprepared, vulnerable and empty. There were so many questions. Who was she? What was left of her? Would she just self-destruct? She didn't feel strong enough to handle the next day. Her armor had shattered.

Underneath her nun's habit was someone she didn't know anymore. She was looking for some remnants of the girl she used to be. Looking in the mirror she had to convince herself that it wasn't the devil looking back at her, just a very distorted picture of herself. After she shed this comfort of the religious blanket around her and peeled off every last layer – she felt naked, freezing, stripped of her dignity and pride. Whoever she was, at last she could be true to herself.

Somehow the decision was made by someone above. Diana liked thinking that, just in case it was another mistake of hers. She had to leave. How could she stay? She could not even allow the fact that this would probably break her mother's heart, deter her. She by now had considered her a half a saint. It would severely test her beliefs, too – and hopefully not shatter them. Later her sister told her that this shock of her departure from the convent was very necessary for their mother. It brought her back to reality. Diana had no idea. No one ever told her how her life had affected anyone else in her family. Her mother apparently had worked herself into a fanatic religious frenzy, living a "Saint's" life herself as an obligation to God for granting her such a great honor as to have a daughter chosen for this holy cause. She had alienated the rest of the family, and isolated herself in excessive and unrealistic religious commitments and practices, demanding the same from everyone around her.

Diana hoped that her return to "normal life" and normal standards freed her from the tremendous pressure she felt.

When Diana announced her decision to leave at the convent in fall that year, everyone was stunned. She learned that the General Mother Superior, the head of the Order, was coming from Rome, their headquarters, and her sole purpose was to see her and try to "save" her. When she heard this she packed her bag immediately. She could not wait for her, she had met her, she I liked her; she would convince her to stay. It was common knowledge how the Superior at the previous location had hated and insanely tortured her for three years. She told her Superiors that she could never handle this again.

To take her final vows was total submission to any Superior. If she stayed she would accept that. It was all or nothing. She was either going to be the best nun, or no nun. She had to make a choice. Really it felt like she had no choice. The decision was made. She had to leave. After that was clear to her, no one could change her mind. She surprised herself. Even after they promised her she would never again encounter such treatment, she told them she was leaving. Of course that was not half the story. She could not bear to tell them about the other horrors. She couldn't speak of this to anyone. In the confessional she looked to God for understanding. She tried to explain, to find answers to what she should do - and she couldn't find the words.

The superior who accosted her would write her Christmas cards for years, even long after she had left the convent. Diana didn't know why she still felt intimidated and obligated to write back, even though she cringed every time on the few words she could find. She figured she might be sorry and very troubled. Surely she knew what she had done to her was wrong. How Diana had learned to make excuses! She absorbed the blame. She wanted to absolve her, forgive her. She wasn't that kind to herself. Her religious upbringing and the convent had taught her not to carry bitterness toward others in her heart, and she tried not to place any blame on anyone other than herself. She was tortured deep down to her core – carrying guilt and blame for everything and everyone.

Yet, on the outside, she had learned to pretend. She had to pretend! She pretended to be on top of the world for a day at a time. She was brave. This was no time to cry. Life went on regardless, like a machine, running...

Diana had to be 60 years old to come to terms with the fact that, yes, there was blame to be placed, and it was not hers to carry. Of course, if one absolved everyone else, one was left with oneself, because someone was accountable and responsible. Even writing this in its first draft, Diana just glossed over it all, being so nice about everyone. One might have thought she lived among Saints. She had no loyalty to herself. She saw now that throughout her life her loyalties were often misplaced. As she delved deep into her soul now she found a giant sleeping. She finally allowed herself to get angry and to set the record straight. Yes, there were wrongs, and Diana placed responsibility on the figures and institutions of authority in her life, especially religion; they betrayed her innocence, they left her intimidated and defenseless and open to harm, they impaired her judgment and stole her freedom of choice.

Diana left the convent. She made that choice. It was the hardest thing she had ever done. For a long time she didn't know that she had any choices. She didn't even realize that she wanted freedom. She didn't know what freedom was. It felt like a relief to have made the decision. There it was - that final fortitude her parents had left her, the spirit she was born with, the drive to survive and rebel. At times in her life when she was totally fenced in, her free spirit would suddenly break out. Her tremendous sense of pride surfaced again – and it allowed her to at least hold up her head with some remnant of dignity. She realized that pride wasn't the worst thing. She had totally renounced this "devilish" trait in the convent, like she was supposed to do. Now she found she needed it to survive. In her search for basic values she found that pride is a very special commodity.

It was like gold – you can bury it, mutilate and try to destroy it; somehow it would surface again – shining…

She found the strength to change the course of her life.

Diana had seen her family twice in ten years. She thought she must be "dead to the world" by now. No one would remember her, nor care.

Shortly before her departure from the convent Diana was given 200 DM (approximately $100.00) to buy herself some clothes to wear for the "outside world". She was lost in the store her very first time shopping, but she would learn this and many other things. She bought a gray sweater and skirt (three sizes too big), and a pair of shoes. When she had returned from that shopping trip, the nuns laughed at her because she had wandered through the "bad" part of the city, the quarter that the prostitutes occupied. No wonder people were hanging out the windows and staring at her. Not that she comprehended what prostitutes were, but she remembered being very embarrassed. Later she wanted to scream! Could you imagine a nun walking the streets? Then she just wondered if she could survive in this scary world out there.

The few belongings she had fit into a small bag. When that door closed behind her she felt like she was let out of jail to stand in the middle of an endless desert – one alternative as scary as the other. She had been given train-fair home. Diana did not know what made her vomit – the smell of the smoky train or the hopelessness of destination. It made her think of her brother on his way to Siberia. She wished that day that the train would never stop. Diana hated trains ever since.

She felt numb. Her mind traveled backwards… to her childhood. She was looking for a safe place. Of course she couldn't find one there either, only the sound of boots rang in her ears.

Accustomed to having very modest expectations of life, she told herself that she must not deserve a better future. She told herself that she had no regrets, that there was no blame. Of course there were consequences, but she would handle them, she told herself. Life was full of adversity, character was branded under fire, emotions tested, crippled... but this all was supposed to make one strong, she told herself. Those were the meager facts. That was life. Look at her parents' life. In her mind she certainly did not deserve more.

Only after this ten-year long "time served", ten more years of "kneeling on firewood" in this convent - Diana realized the disabling effects they had on her. If she buried this part of her life deep enough in her soul, maybe someday it would be wiped out forever? Not so. She knew she would be debriefing for years. Not until that day though was she able to assess the damage, the lack of a normal developmental process she was robbed of, and the immensely confusing emotions that battered her immature life. Most destructive of all were the betrayal of her high ideals, the betrayal of the innocence of a child so wide open and hungry for all the good and the beautiful, and a simple chance to be something great...

Diana didn't keep one picture of anyone nor of herself from this time of her life. She never wanted to look back. She thought she could just close this chapter of her life; close another chapter of her life... If only it was that simple.

For many years to come – the convent would haunt her. In her nightmares she would always lose everyone and everything that was dear to her in her entire life, and she would end up back in the convent. God would punish her...

She felt that she would never be allowed any peace. She felt cursed. It was like this huge hole that would suck her down into the deep…a magnetic force pulling her back… She felt like sinking.

Throughout her life she questioned her choice. Had she broken her promise to God? Would he punish her for "going back on her word"? Had she reneged on her commitment to serve him in the convent? She had arrived at a dead-end road. She didn't know that she was allowed any other choices. Was there no other life for her? That's what ten years of convent culture would impress on anyone's mind.

Diana certainly had sincere intentions. It was hard for her to distinguish what her place was in the world, to separate reality from fiction. It would take some time to untie her jumbled-up emotions. She prayed that God would tell her what she was intended to be… She had nightmares for years. Was she ever going to find peace and resolve?

Only in a distant corner of her heart she heard a little voice telling her that she had a right to be, a right to even be her, a right to be free…

VI

FOREIGN   WATERS

Collecting the pieces and starting over was like teaching a bird with broken wings to fly. It was a foreign world all together. It took some recovery, a luxury Diana knew she couldn't afford. She didn't have time for it. She had to get on her feet in a hurry. She needed to eat.

She certainly was a child at twenty-five. So she was poor once again, stripped not only of everything, of a roof over her head and food to eat, but now also of herself, her pride, her dignity, her confidence, her idealism, her religion, her emotions. She was too raw to feel anything – She could not allow herself to feel… She didn't have time to cry.

Every night she had a different nightmare, running away from this person with a wide mouth full of huge teeth… the sound of the drums…the boots…the convent - over and over. In leaving the convent she had made a conscious decision to jump into the waters of the real world, but did she know how to swim? No. Did she know just how foreign these waters were? She was ill-equipped, and so naïve. She had been detached and sheltered from reality for too long. She actually was afraid of facing people, of acting inappropriately in public. She felt like apologizing for being there, out of place…

It was a foregone conclusion that she was not going home to her parents. She couldn't even imagine what she would say to them. Instead she showed up at her sister Elli's place in Munich. In the worst crisis situations during her life, when she couldn't talk to anyone, Diana would always turn to her. Once or twice when she was really stranded she ended up on her doorstep. There were no questions. She would always be there with open arms. Diana needed a safe place, a place with no judgement. Thinking of her sister, a light went on in her soul. She always saw the good in everyone. Would she still see her as her little sister, and still "cover her face in the rain, so she wouldn't get freckles?" She was sunshine, she was fresh air. She found the silver lining. And she did. She let her sleep for days…She let her be…There were no questions, just open arms… and a time to debrief. Diana needed a lifetime of that. This was one of the most devastating times of her life. She stayed with her sister for a couple of weeks. She had no clothes, no money, no confidence or much of anything else. Elli pulled out her sewing machine and showed her how to sew a brown dress for herself, the only dress she owned for some time. She gave her back a few of her childhood pictures. She gave her back some sense of her identity. She gave her time and space without judgement or control. She let her heal. She let her be. She always rescued her. "Like the day I lost you", she laughed, "and looked for you all over town." When Diana was two years old, Elli had to pick berries behind their house for potato strudel, and she thought Diana was asleep. Instead she climbed out of her crib onto the windowsill, opened the window and screamed 'til a neighbor walking by rescued her and took her to his house. Her sister couldn't find her. Her mother came home and there was no baby. They found her a few hours later. Another day Diana took her cat for a walk outside in her doll buggy. She was barely walking. When the cat ran away she followed her for a mile down the road. That time someone brought her home and they both got in trouble. Diana remembered her singing to her when she was little…"Kommt ein Vogerl", "Hanschen klein", Fuchs, Du hast die Gans gestohlen" and "Schlaf, Kindchen, schlaf"…She was always singing.

Elli said that Diana was always running away. They said she was a lot of trouble. Her big brother Frank, babysitting, was a disaster. He would only play his guitar loud enough to drown out her screaming. And her brother Jo made her crazy just by making funny faces at her. So, Elli was it. Elli was always there. She was the best.

Diana envied her sister. Somehow she wondered why her sister had not lost her faith, her humor and trust in people, and her fortitude. Because she endured poverty worse than her. They always said Diana was the spoiled little runt that came along when things were already much better than during their childhood years. Diana was eleven years younger than her. Elli had also encountered the war times, with both her brothers off in the wars, hardship and hard work from childhood on, and then the early death of her husband. Their little girl, her pride and joy, they named after her. Diana felt so honored. It meant that she had missed her, too.

Within two weeks Diana had found a job ad for a Registered Nurse in the newspaper in a northern city of Germany, far away again. Somehow, distance seemed a comfort. Was it that she couldn't face herself - or face anyone else? Was it that she needed to find herself first?

She applied and got the job. She had to give references from the convent, to account for all those years of her life. She was reluctant to do so. The convent did not give her any references. She felt so odd and thought that she would never fit in anywhere. She faked her way through it. She had poor communication skills and was socially inept, to say the least. Other than the clothes on her back and two RN uniforms she was penniless.

Diana visited her parents then for a few days, informing them of her new job. Her sister Elli accompanied her, and she was so glad to have her with her to diffuse the tension. They were all hurting for her. She couldn't stand everyone's pain and sympathy. She never wanted to fall back on her parents. And then there were her mother's eyes…they looked right through her, knowingly, haunting her, as though she knew that something unspeakable had happened. She could not tell. She would never tell.

Her first apartment, a studio room at the new hospital, had nothing in it but a pullout bed. It was comforting this way, just four walls around her; they were not the only things that were bare and naked. She couldn't have handled more. She needed to feel free.

…And coming up for air...

Diana had never been dancing, to a prom or on a date. She had never listened to a love song on the radio, had never watched a movie on TV. She was a twenty-five-year-old adult. She was a child. She felt handicapped… She needed to rebuild from scratch. Never did she forget her first paycheck in her entire life. Suppose one would say this. For her it was a milestone. She was twenty-five years old, and had never been rewarded with anything. It was the first reality, the concrete proof in her hands that told her that she was worth something, and that she would make it. Counting on her basic sense of survival – her parents' legacy - she knew that if she worked hard she would get on her feet again, and nothing could stop her or hold her down for long. She was resilient. She would bounce back. She had been strong once.

Were her broken wings strong enough to fly?

The sun came up in the morning once more, and the cherry tree started to bloom again. Diana crocheted a pillow and a doily; she bought herself a yellow candle and a vase for flowers, not for roses or exotic ones, but for just a few stems of grasses. She would be OK. It was something she did for nothing else and no one else but for herself – this child, an entity, a person all by herself, that – with baby steps – was learning how to walk... Frantically she was searching for her own identity, her place in this new world. Did she have "likes", or a favorite thing, or a specific taste of her own? Or was she "cultured" to be whatever was expected of her, to blend with the surroundings, the "normal", not to stick out like a sore thumb? Had she conceded her identity, traded it for anonymity, to survive in a crowd?

Diana needed to find the person she was. She had to get back to basics, to see the beauty in simplicity, to rediscover the pure joy of being alive.

She bought herself a radio. Only she couldn't decide what era of music she liked... Having missed ten years of her life was much like being in a coma while the rest of the world moved on. She felt like a foreigner in a strange country. It was a traumatic realization for her that she didn't know any "modern" music, any songs anyone else was enjoying. She loved music. She needed music to heal. Most of the sparse music of her childhood she had forgotten. It was war music, outdated. No one sang church music in this setting. The religious songs she knew seemed inappropriate in the "world" - settings she was trying to fit into. Even though she played her radio every spare minute, there was a big hole in her heart... She didn't know any songs. Would she ever learn how to dance?

Sometimes she felt like she was floating without a direction in a world too overwhelming, a world so translucent and foreign and just too big for her.

Diana didn't really know who she was. She tried to hide her convent history from everyone. She was embarrassed by her ignorance. The nurses and superiors were extremely nice to her and almost too kind... They knew she was a child from another planet. She tried desperately, too desperately, to fit in and behave like everyone else. Only she was afraid of letting anyone get too close to her.

After his discharge, a patient of hers returned one day with a gift for her: an entire "forest" of flowers, leaves and berries from Holland...There was no vase big enough, and it ended up in this lovely huge milk can in the hospital foyer. It was the most gorgeous gift she ever received; it was the only gift she ever received as an adult. It validated her. It changed her course. She was "a good nurse", the card said... All the nurses and even the hospital administrator came up to her and acknowledged it. This was a lifeline! Diana knew she was a good nurse. She had something of worth after all, she wasn't a bad person, and she could help and serve and heal and comfort others, and forget about herself... Servitude was the only thing she considered herself faintly good at. She will never forget the kind gesture of this patient. It helped her enormously. She would make it – She could move on and forget the past. She would survive.

Diana could hear her mother say, "Don't waste time crying over spilled milk".

There would be a tomorrow.

She was just setting roots at her new job when a letter came from a guy she went to grammar school with. He had heard that she had left the convent, and Diana's parents gave him her address. Diana trusted that they wouldn't give her address to just anyone. He said that he always liked her in school, and always thought they'd get together later. She didn't expect any man even looking at her. Maybe she was flattered that someone actually remembered her from ten years ago. How is that for picking up where she had left off! The only connection or attraction – if you will – was that he came from the same town, same time, same era, that he didn't mind that she had been in the convent... Also - that he had a worse childhood than she did – because he had a stepmother that half beat him to death. The entire town knew that – and Diana always felt sorry for him.

Anyway, his letter came from the U.S.A., his cousin had sponsored him, and he himself had been in the U.S.A. for less than a year. This made an impression on Diana. It impressed her that he had ventured out of their small hometown. It brought back very fond memories of the Americans after the war, the packages from her cousin from the U.S.A., even her dreams from long ago of a bigger, better, freer world – a child's dreams, long expunged by the ten years of a totally opposite mentality in a convent.

Several weeks after his letter he came to Germany on a vacation, just to see her. She was bewildered and felt obligated to pick him up at the harbor and visit their families with him. Of course she quit her job to have the time. He would tell her later that he was very disappointed that she didn't run to him and throw her arms around him, overjoyed to see him. She didn't understand his disappointment. She didn't even know him. She blamed herself that she wasn't capable of feeling such exuberance. She didn't question that his expectations were bizarre.

On their car rides, while visiting their families, they had many senseless and pointless arguments. She remembered being so embarrassed visiting his sister that really didn't want to have anything to do with them, or spent even five minutes with them, while he insisted to stay at her place. She remembered crying in the car. Then they visited his brother in a mental hospital. Her parents weren't too thrilled, but weren't going to interfere, after all –her father had given him her address. He seemed OK, they thought. Diana went to work at a hospital in Passau in the meantime. After his vacation of four weeks he gave her a ring –before he left.

By that time Diana had decided to cross the ocean to the U.S.A., filed her immigration papers: her mother's cousin in Chicago would sponsor her. Why not? What was keeping her in Germany? It wasn't her home anymore; she had no base anywhere, no friends... only a disappointed and disillusioned family. She really didn't belong. Her parents had moved from their hometown to Passau and were living at her oldest sister's house they helped build. She didn't know a soul there. She had no roots there. She had no place there and no one expected her to stay. She felt like she was a fugitive, running and running. She knew that she did not belong.

Diana thought all these events falling into place must be God's will, as they seemed to develop without much of her doing. There must be a purpose in it...Perhaps there was another life for her, another chance to do it right...She always used to believe that all things happen for a reason, for a greater purpose one might understand later, and that things or people are just instruments to get one there. Perhaps she would understand that purpose later. It must be God's will. Her entire life was so far controlled by others .She was accustomed to follow. Who had a choice? For now it was easier to blame it on God. She couldn't handle any more guilt.

The rest was also automatic. She flew to the USA. She had never even been in an airplane before. It all seemed like a dream. Her sister had dropped her off at the airport in Munich, and on the way had told her that her mother's cousin in Chicago withdrew the sponsorship when she found out that she was coming to be with her boyfriend. So she landed in Chicago as an illegal immigrant and couldn't get a Green Card without a sponsor. For several weeks she was petrified of getting deported. It started to sink in that this time she was really "homeless", this time she was "between" two countries, a "fugitive" from one, a foreigner - an illegal one at that - in the other... As a child she always found it strange living "between two towns, not "belonging" to either.

It was clear to her that no matter what soil she was standing on, it wasn't free. Her father would say: "Wer nicht arbeiten will, soll auch nicht essen", meaning: "No work, no eat". It was all up to her. She knew no one. She needed a job, yesterday!

For weeks they couldn't find a sponsor for her. They knew very few people. At last her boyfriend's boss was so kind as to sponsor her. She was forever grateful. Now she was committed to make this work.

Her boyfriend had no money, nor did he have a care in the world. He had found himself evicted when he had returned from his vacation a few weeks earlier, but he didn't seem to care, or to try and look for an apartment. He refused to leave that German couple's home, and slept in their stairway on a cot. When Diana arrived, they let her sleep on their living room couch for a week until she insisted that they find a room. Her boyfriend said that they couldn't live together unless they were married, and her values demanded no less. Three weeks from the date Diana arrived in the U.S.A. they were married at St. Gregory Catholic Church. It was the "right thing" to do.

A couple of weeks later Diana missed her period. She already had taken a job at Edgewater Hospital, and they moved his 12-inch black-and-white television, his bike and his car payment to their small apartment.

Diana never heard from the cousin that withdrew the sponsorship, and she made no effort to contact her for years. Two of her cousin's brothers and a sister with family were living in Chicago also, Diana found out later. They knew she was in Chicago. She made their acquaintance a long time later.

Diana worked in the nursery at the hospital, and she remembered struggling with the language, the conversions of baby weights, measurements and medications – being used to the metric system (not used here at that time). A couple of months later she bettered herself by taking a job at Bethany Hospital with a good pay increase and her professional license being applied for. The Hospital Administrator was very kind. Diana liked her job there, and she worked throughout her pregnancy, and part-time later.

Sometimes Diana thought about it. Events followed like links in a chain, pulling her in all directions. It seemed like so many things happened overnight, without her doing, like she was caught up in a whirlwind – just spinning along…Suddenly she was married and pregnant, when a year ago she was still in the convent…

Today, of course, she asked herself: "What was the matter with me? What was the rush? Why didn't I stop to think?" Oh, who was she to think? Then it was about survival, and about the "proper thing to do".

There were social and religious models… A girl grew up to get married. She had already deviated from the norm by her ten-year tenure in a convent, which wasn't very complimentary for a girl. It wasn't socially acceptable or fashionable for a girl to be alone in any setting. There would have to be something seriously wrong with you, you were totally ugly or ill or difficult if you couldn't marry. A spinster was a disgrace.

There was, of course, the religious model: The family, God's purpose for creation all together. The unity of two people was completion; the purpose of marriage was re-creation. In her time there were a father, a mother and children.

There was no talk about independence or individuality or personal freedom for a woman, not where she came from. It wasn't a question of what a woman wanted. She didn't know what she wanted anyway, or who she was. She didn't know that it was OK to love herself or how to value herself…She didn't know that one could be complete and fulfilled being alone… She didn't know many things.

The abuse in their marriage started immediately. Diana was belted right after they had moved into their apartment. With the three hundred dollars her parents had given her for her return flight to Germany (if she should need it), they bought a sleeper couch, because they had no bed. They used a cardboard box for a table, and Diana made a little tablecloth to cover it all up…

Should she have taken that plane back to Germany? Going back? She never considered going back a choice. She was committed to their marriage. It was a sacrament. She had made enough mistakes. This time she would do it right, she was married now; even her parents would respect that. She would make them proud yet.

Her mother sent her a feather comforter all the way from Germany. That was the customary wedding gift for a girl from her parents, a parting gift when she left home. Even though she had left home long ago, it was not to get married. Her sisters were given their comforter and it was important to her parents to do the same for her. She never expected her parents to give her anything. The comforter was a sign that they had accepted her status. On the other hand it was clear to her that their parental obligation was fulfilled. It drove home the point of "You made your bed, you lie in it." It didn't hurt too much now, because Diana felt abandoned long ago…

She remembered considering jumping from their third-floor window while her new husband was chasing and belting her around the apartment, the only way to make him stop - a hairline away from desperation. She had not made the "right" dinner when he came home drunk at 3 A.M. from work, or rather his stop at the tavern. She would cook the pork chops he wanted; and then get up for work at the hospital at 5A.M. - after sex, the "wifely duty"- another woman's lot like the period and every other humiliating thing a woman was for. She didn't know any foreplay or an orgasm during her 15-year marriage. She thought sexual pleasure was for a man; a woman was just his instrument, his property. She thought it was wrong to expect happiness in life or to experience joy. In her culture the pursuit of pleasure was considered selfish and reprehensible. Romance or chemistry were just dreams, and not in the stars for everyone. They were certainly foreign to her. Life was supposed to be hardship; it was surviving, and if one was lucky, escaping death. It almost seemed a sacrilege to expect to be happy in life. What perfect soil for planting abuse.

Her daughter asked her what gave her this "respect for life" that prevented her from jumping that day – considering that her childhood was full of death and destruction, and her life since destined to end up in one disaster after another. Was it respect for life? That is too kind. She thought of it as fear of God, fear of death and hell. She was too much of a coward. She couldn't kill a fly, much less herself.

She became pregnant, and now there was no way back, no way out. Not that she didn't want that baby. She remembered her oldest sister loving her babies to pieces, even in the hardest times. Diana worked well into her eighth month of pregnancy. When her husband dropped her off at the Emergency Room - in labor - and went back to work, she thought it was normal. There was no one to hold her hand, no one to comfort her throughout the twenty-four-hour labor. She didn't know any better. She didn't expect or deserve any more. She was a subservient and "easy wife" to have. Her husband became comfortable with that.

Soon Diana realized that this baby was the most precious gift she ever had. It was totally dependent on her. She would protect her child; she would love it and enjoy it, if alone. She wrote poems for her baby about "the soul smiling out of baby's eyes," She remembered. This pure innocence made the whole ugly world go away. That baby would be a beautiful person someday. Perhaps there was a worthwhile purpose in her life after all. Maybe she'd get a stab at being something great, maybe the best mother ever. She valued her life now, because this baby needed her. It was her reason to carry on.

The first toy she bought her was a teddy bear, something her parents could never afford when she was a child. She believed that her daughter kept it all her life. She would have a good life, that baby, much better than hers.

Of course, motherhood didn't come with instructions. There was no Owner's Manual. There should have been. It was not too hard for her, being of a resourceful and practical nature. It was not hard to love a baby! She figured things out and learned quickly. No one told her that motherhood did amazing things to you. She had no idea how much it could change ones entire world overnight, how it added another dimension to one's life. It felt like she grew another heart, another sense the instant her baby was born. She would hear it breathing day and night, every second, wherever she was. It was like she was whole, finally complete and connected to this other being. She learned to do things she never imagined. She cleaned up messes she never thought possible. She realized that one would jump over and crawl under to move mountains for one's child. Her baby was the best, the smartest, the cutest ever born, and her diapers didn't smell. She would defend it against dragons and goblins with hugs and kisses - and against the world with her life. She would be as strong as she needed to be. After long days and sleepless nights she miraculously would find energy for a bedtime story, and she would fly her child on a magic carpet around the world of endless possibilities she never dreamed of before.

Diana's own hopes and dreams and thoughts and actions were now centered on her child. She became whatever it took to mother her child. She became her best. She forget herself, a reward of motherhood…

No one told Diana any of this. She was on cloud nine for a while. She felt alive!

Oh, the dreams she had!

Would her mother say: "Beware…?" Deep down in her soul some cautious little voices kept whispering and warning that really she didn't deserve so much joy. She had already used up too many graces. What did she have to do not to jinx her good fortune? She remembered sitting by the baby's crib some nights, crying and telling her baby all her troubles. Who else could she tell that she really was exhausted from trying to be the perfect mother! Could she expose that she was more vulnerable than she had ever been in her life? No one could ever know that behind the scenes were a lonesome emptiness, depletion, isolation and loss of the little self she knew. By the standards of her time it was not ok to complain. One would have been a terrible mother if one couldn't handle it. It would have been a sin.

Diana admired the liberated mothers that were not ashamed to admit to the struggles and woes every mother knew well, every mother, her mother, she, her daughters, mothers of all times…

And in the end the rewards and the joys of motherhood prevail, and one may want another child…and do it all over again.

A few days after they brought the baby home, a priest that lived across the hall came over, supposedly to congratulate them, or bless the baby. She was sleeping in the crib. He picked the baby up and threw her up in the air. Diana held her breath. She thought she was going to slap him, she wanted to scream, but she couldn't speak. She grabbed the baby and went into the other room but she said nothing.

Diana had not yet learned that freedom. She was too intimidated. He was a priest! She just took the baby from him and went into the other room, hating herself for not having the guts to tell him off, throw him out, have him committed, arrested. She blamed herself for a long time for not knowing how to properly handle a situation like this. She felt like a coward.

From then on no one touched that baby! Diana never trusted anyone. They never had a babysitter.

And she grew up with her baby.

Her husband loved the baby, too, in his own way and as much as he was capable of. If he didn't know how to love, it was because he wasn't loved as a baby. His mother died at his birth, and even later he told the kids that he always thought he "killed his mother". His stepmother certainly had no love for him and abused him terribly. How would he know how to love? Diana always had felt sorry for him. She thought she would try to be extra good and love him double to help him overcome that void.

She always had this incessant drive to jump in and help anyone in need, to heal and to serve… This priority to put any cause before her own, whether inherited or acquired through her life culture didn't always serve her well. However selfless, charitable and even rewarding this may seem – even while satisfying religious and/or moral obligations, it became a misguided and misused need. Diana had no loyalty to herself. She had never learned to value herself.

Times were hard for them. "Happiness" was not in their vocabulary. Diana became accustomed to abuse. She didn't feel that she deserved any better. Her husband was always sorry afterwards, always sorry, an expert at apologies. It usually entitled him to a making-up/love-making episode rewarding him for being so sorry. He was an alcoholic and definitely had a mental problem. She felt sorry for him.

They tried to make it work. Diana tried to subordinate herself like a wife was supposed to do. The husband was the boss, and a good wife was to love and obey and do what she was told. She had to fight with her alcoholic husband to make rational decisions, where to live, the care of the children, money matters…They couldn't even have an intelligent disagreement. Someone had to make rational decisions. It was very hard for her.

Why did God give her a brain and a will of her own, if she wasn't allowed to use it? Diana hated her intelligence. She blamed herself for not being what she was supposed to be. After all, marriage was a sacred commitment. She needed to conform, and she tried. Especially after her parents had told him, he said, that she was difficult and stubborn, and "good luck" trying to break her. It wouldn't surprise her if her parents really said that. She was raised in a culture in which a woman had no rights. She just never could get that through her head. Any kind of freedom for a woman would have been considered arrogance. A "good woman" was one that followed rules. She was a servant. She was expected to succumb to the man's wishes and directions. No brains required. A "good woman" had no voice, no choice, and no say. She always put herself last. That was honorable. That was a "good woman". Why wasn't she a man?

Diana often wondered how her mother ever lived up to that image. She certainly was considered a "good woman", and her father was the boss. However, while he presented this image to the world and to his children, she knew that in private her mother's wish was his command. It was obvious that he loved and respected her above all, and she in turn was as smart as she was diplomatic to not let even him think for a moment that he wasn't the boss.

Diana herself had lived many years of this same selfless and honorable life in the convent. She was used to sacrifice. She had been chastised for "wanting" and for having anything "her way". She thought she had learned to curb her needs and wants. Yet it never felt fair. Wasn't there any place in this world where a woman was given an equal chance? What dignity was there in living if one was not allowed a choice? Deep down in her soul she still harbored rebellious thoughts that someday her turn would come when she would be allowed to have an opinion of her own, to decide for herself, to her own success or mistakes, to have a choice in a matter. She still had the devil in her. Her spirit seemed invincible.

Her husband swore he was going to "break" her, "tame" her, he called it, like a wild horse. For her own good he was going to straighten her out.

All her life everyone was always interested in "her own good". Perhaps they were right. Perhaps her husband was right. She had made enough mistakes. She wanted to trust him. She couldn't trust her judgement. Her low self-esteem, the fear of the authority of husband/marriage, and feeling sorry for him was really a lethal combination.

The abuse continued. She let it continue…

This low self-esteem was cultured throughout every phase of Diana's life; it wasn't likely going to improve at this point. She let it disable her and chain her spirit. It had more than one reason, this low self-worth of hers. God only knows how much guilt she carried around with her. Here she wanted to be a good and obedient wife while she really felt like a hypocrite hiding a terrible secret that haunted her in her dreams.

How could she ever tell her husband that during the last week before she left Germany she "got herself raped" – due to her incredible stupidity – like all rape victims believe? A few of her old grammar school classmates saw her in a restaurant in her hometown. They bought her two glasses of wine, and she was drunk. She had never had an alcoholic beverage before in her life. One of the guys walked her home and raped her in the middle of the snow-packed road. Diana couldn't talk about all her life. All she remembered thinking was that she wanted to die right at that spot.

She was so ashamed for not being smart enough to know better, to prevent things like this from happening to her. She had never had any sex education nor allowed herself "sinful thoughts" about the subject. The act itself confused her. She felt retarded. She had no clue. She hated herself. She learned that ignorance is no excuse, and innocence shouldn't be confused with protection. She learned the hard way.

How could she ever tell anyone? She could never tell her husband. He was belting her now, what would he do if he knew this? He would blame her, and God knows what else. She was his possession, and she was tainted. He would have never understood, nor forgiven her. Instead she buried it deep in her soul, the only safe place – like all the other nightmares of her life.

She was not allowed to keep her secret to herself. Her husband's stepmother would not let her forget it. She wrote him, informing him of this guy from their hometown bragging that he had "robbed her of her virginity," before she left Germany, claiming another notch in his belt.

Her husband was furious because he was jealous that he might not have been the first - a competitive issue, hurting his male pride. She may not have been a virgin! He would have never believed that she had been violated, nor would he have cared. Even if she had admitted it he would have been furious only at her, never at the guy, a buddy of his.

In Diana's hometown no one thought of rape. Guys thought it their right to lay every woman they could get their hands on, which attests to their primitive mentality, no less than the subhuman and uncivilized moral culture in that town with respect to women.

She lied and lied; and his stepmother kept writing... It was a long-term issue. Diana accepted it as her fault; she felt she deserved all of her husband's anger. This part of her life was still raw. She has been working on laying it to rest ever since.

There was no love. They survived; she carried on day after day, year after year. They had another child. For a little while she felt like she stole a little happiness. Yet nothing changed in their marriage, in their lives. If it wasn't for the children, her reason for being, she didn't know how she would have done it. Her life was devoted to them. They were her purpose in life, the reason for her to carry on. She would do whatever it took. So she put everything she had into fixing things she had control over, and her children.

They couldn't pay the rent and live on her husband's salary. While she was on pregnancy leave she worked for an old shop down on Clark street sewing eyeglass-cases for $1.50/hr., until her body was raw from flea bites. It forced her to go back to Nursing and take her State Boards. As a foreign nurse she still couldn't' get her R.N. License in Illinois until she had completed a semester in Psychiatric Nursing at the Chicago State Mental Hospital. Besides struggling with the English language and medical terminology, she had to take the bus all the way through the city, which made her sick every day. Oh, the bus! Her nursing job was waiting for her. It paid more money, and the rewards of being able to make a difference in her patients' lives were enormous for her. She got more than she gave, she kept saying.

Diana was a good nurse. It fit her personality. There were times when she had trouble separating herself, staying professional and detached enough not wanting to die with every cancer patient, or cry while treating a sick child…

That was her – wanting to take her psychiatric patients home with her, wanting to adopt every abused and abandoned child, wanting to take on everyone's problems and stop all the wrongs, all the pain and misery in the world…

Like she said – she got more than she gave. Everyone's heart is full of something. Compassion took up enough space in hers not to leave much for herself. That was her salvation.

After moving from apartment to apartment for years, Diana persuaded her husband to buy a small house, a very small house. He was very opposed to the idea of having such a great

152

responsibility, but was also tired of moving. She borrowed $ 4,000.00 for the down payment from her mother's cousin in Chicago that she had never met before. She worked part-time to pay it back promptly. She didn't know how to drive yet, and had to take the bus to work or walk several miles. So she finally learned to drive. She cleaned and painted and fixed up the house, sewed all their clothes, made the drapes and whatever. She painted the bedroom set the previous owners had left for them - a bright yellow color. The kids could walk to the Catholic school. Their house was the playground for all the neighborhood kids. They had paints and toys all over. They lived with their record player and all the American children's songs…along came Sesame Street, thank God… They even took in a two-year-old child; she can't remember how that happened. Her mother worked at Kodak. That's all she knew about them. Little Andy was with them for about a year, like she belonged to them. Her mother was single and Diana never asked her to pay anything. She felt sorry for her because she was single and obviously had to struggle. It could happen to her.

Shortly after they had moved into their house she became pregnant with their third child. It had been a fight trying any measures of birth control. Her cycle was very irregular. Her doctor had allowed her to take birth control pills for six month to regulate her cycle. She had to hide them because her husband was opposed to all birth control; he just wanted his sex whenever he was ready. She had her own scruples. They really could not afford another child. Diana had secretly talked to priests and doctors to let her continue her prescription a little longer several times. The doctors said that it wasn't safe or indicated. The priests told her it was a sin, and on her own conscience, her tortured conscience.

The superstition Diana remembered from home did not help her either: "When you move into a new home, either there has to be an addition to the family - or a person in the house moves out (dies)". It was just possible that God would punish her this way.

So she tried to hold things together, and look forward to a new baby. She had just started a new job as an industrial nurse, and was so grateful that her new boss didn't fire her when she told him she was pregnant just after she had started. He was a kind man. There were no maternity leaves, etc. then and she was allowed to work into her eighth month. She was a sweetheart, that little baby from day one, and Diana thanked God for her to this day. However, even the new baby did not "fix" their marriage, nor did happiness move into their home. Anyway, many years, many tears, and three beautiful children later, their life had not changed. There was no love... they tried for another year...She'd hear her mother say: "You should be ashamed to complain." So she would thank God that no worse disasters befell them. They were alive. There were people that lost a child or were ill. She should not be ungrateful. It gave her the strength to move on another day...

They had a cat, and one Christmas they even bought a collie. Tiger, "jumped the fence" a year later. Diana didn't have the heart to tell the kids until they were grown up, that she had to have him put to sleep because he had bitten some neighborhood kids. She couldn't handle it herself very well.

There always was a cat around for most of her life from the time when she was very little until now – a friend in good and bad times, especially when she was sad or couldn't sleep at night. The kids would bring home a sick bird, another dog, and every animal one can think of, at one time or another...

Diana taught her children all she knew…She taught them to play the piano, the organ…She made sure they all learned how to swim. It was important to her that they were not afraid of water like she was. She made Halloween costumes, Puppet theatres, Birthday cakes and Christmas decorations. They performed Christmas plays with their friends for the parents and teachers and the school. She taught them to sing, to pray, to bake, and paint. In summer they had First Aid classes for children. She worked at the school office in the morning to pay her dues and stay involved with the children's progress, fighting with the teachers for fair treatment. They were making things and creating, and being busy. Some of it was not easy, because she herself had never flown a kite, carved a pumpkin, never been camping, skating or fishing, she didn't know hopscotch. She had to first learn the National Anthem before she could teach it to them. She learned. She tried to relive her childhood the way she wished it would have been. It would carry her through this time. The children would have a better life someday. She would do everything in her power to see to that. Their children were very talented. They would save money for their college education…she had no idea how… It wasn't one of her husband's ambitions. He felt that no one had helped him to get any education; therefore the children should fend for themselves as well.

The house, the yard, and pretty much everything else were her responsibility. She raced through the day like there was no tomorrow. She couldn't allow herself to relax. God forbid she'd have time to think! How often she begged her husband to run an errand, to teach their son to cut the lawn, or rake the leaves. Later she found out that he rather would take the kids to "play pool" at the tavern…

Before she went to work in the evening she would cook dinner, have the house in order and the shopping done, etc. For the rest of the night, while at work, she would worry. Who knows why she had to have the cleanest house even if no one cared but herself – deriving some satisfaction of these menial tasks as the only things she had control over? The importance and significance of this reminded her now of her childhood. It reminded her of her mother's fervent attempts to hold it together, to create a pleasing environment, to bring a sense of order into their otherwise chaotic world.

If anyone had asked her at that time if she was happy, Diana would have said yes, and with a smile, a dead smile…

Somehow she always knew that there was no permanency in their relationship. She always thought she could overcome everything, and fix it. However, there was no love, they were just stranded together.

She was always hoping that tomorrow it would be better.

VII

THE   LESSER   EVIL

Diana wished she could stop right about now.

This was like opening a closet door and have everything fall out at you. Things you hid or forgot you had – and much more junk than you bargained for, things that you saved and stuffed in there to sort and mend and deal with later…

It was time to take it all out, Diana thought, to make sure that no ghosts and skeletons were ever going to surprise her again. It was time to sort it all out, hang things up and put them in place. It was time to decide what was worth keeping – and then throw the rest away…Diana's daughter wondered aloud why she never shared such details while they were growing up. The answer was: "Why? To whose benefit?" Why disturb the muddy waters? She was always taught to just push forward, let things settle, let things lie, don't cry about it. She was driven forward. She had no time to feel sorry for herself. It was too late to cry. Anyway, the fortitude to go forward was the most precious gift she inherited from her parents. She was in awe of their strength and endurance and fortitude and fight for survival in their lifetime. Why should her life be different? She only wished she could be as strong as her parents were.

One conscious reason though for never talking much about her life in her younger years especially, was: not to burden her children with unnecessary baggage that could not benefit them, that may even hinder them and weigh them down, especially while they were little. Her life, where she came from, her past...it was insignificant. She never won a trophy or could boast any heroic deeds or great accomplishments. She wasn't very proud of herself, nor did she expect anyone's sympathy. Her expectations of life were not very high, considering her past culture. She did not consider her tragedies and experiences, such as hunger, slavery, war, rape, etc. any worse than other people's fight for survival. It was all she knew. Her life was nothing special.

As for her children – Diana really didn't want to push their German heritage on them, not because she was not proud of it – her parents, her family. She remembered well, especially when she first came to this country and all her life here, the subtle glances from even the nicest and friendliest people when her German accent gave her away. She always felt so hurt. She was German, but she had not committed Hitler's crimes, it wasn't her fault. She had suffered, too. She would have preferred to be anything but German. This burned a hole in her soul. She wanted to be an American Citizen more than she could say. Her children were born in the U.S.A., thank God. This country was freedom, salvation; it was the chance she wanted all her life, and a chance she never had before... She wished she could have wiped away the stigma of being German.

No, she admitted, she was not proud of her country, her homeland at this time of her life. She was burdened by being German, and it haunted her. "Loyalty" and "Pride" in their "Vaterland" was instilled in them as little children. She wanted to be proud to be German; proud of herself, her family... being so burdened by her German heritage was the ultimate insult to her pride. This was personal. There were many great people in German history; respected people, great composers, world-renowned poets, the famous Bavarian glass artists, painters and artists of all kinds, scientists and more. There was her own family with incredible talents and traits, their spirit and determination and values that were her foundation.

She should be so proud. What was wrong with her?

Her family could not have understood this, she was sure. They were not immigrants to a strange country, either. They did not feel the sting. Germany had changed, too, in the meanwhile, which she wasn't much aware of during her ten convent years, but the Germany she remembered from her childhood had not been too kind to her.

Another reason for not talking much about her life much was her husband. She knew that their children had enough of their own memories. She was not going to perpetuate them. Her husband was a German and proud of it. Only the German image he presented was not anything Diana could be proud of. He used to refer to the "Old Country" with every second breath, often begrudging their children a better life than he had. This justified the disciplinary measures he remembered from his childhood being carried out on their children. Diana could never understand that. Wouldn't you want your children to have a better, a kinder life? The more she wanted to overcome the "old ways", their handicaps, and their inadequate parenting skills as they were, the more insistent he was. There was only one way and that was the German way. There was nothing wrong with the good old ways, they didn't kill him, and they were good enough for their children. All German was Gospel. She often wondered why he wanted to live in the U.S.A., but never wanted to learn the language or the customs of this country. He was and always will be – German. They don't call the Germans "stubborn" for no reason.

Diana thought it was so disrespectful when he and his friends acted this way. If the USA was so bad, why did they live here? She did not want to perpetuate the myth he created that the German way was "the only way" .She loved this new country from the first day she came here. It could only treat them better than the old country she knew. She saw opportunities for her children

159

and herself that she never dreamed of. She wanted more, even though it was wrong and selfish. She needed to move forward. Her husband would say that he was fine living in a hole. He had never had it so good. He had no dreams for a better life. He had no ambitions at all and begrudged any new opportunities that came along. They were like oil and water. They were so different.

Diana didn't encourage the children to learn the German language after they started school. She felt that it was more important that they fit in, and were not handicapped by not knowing the English language. She felt at a disadvantage not being able to teach them so many other things and customs that were second nature to their friends. She had never seen or cooked a turkey before; she didn't know Thanksgiving, or Halloween. Everyone knew she was German when she ate with fork and knife...

They never had many friends. She attempted some friendships, but they never seemed to meet with her husband's approval. He would obviously discourage her friends, and because of this unpleasant environment they wouldn't come over again. It was just as well, because she couldn't allow herself to have a friend. How could she tell a soul about her life behind the scenes? She was ashamed. And she weaved a thicker veil of secrecy over their lives, to protect what little honor she felt she had left... Her loyalties had to be to her husband – as prescribed by their culture. The only people her husband allowed them to associate with or invite to their home were the German friends that he worked with. They would drink heavily and reminisce about the "Old Country", and by evening the men would get carried away. It was often so awkward, but better than staying home and inevitably fighting. Those were the Sundays. The kids hated them. She dreaded them. Sometimes they visited with his friends. She often wondered why these people came to this country. It seemed as though they were a bunch of angry men, unsettled, disgruntled, with sheltered wives and dissatisfied lives. It was a power struggle over who had more dominance over his wife, whose kids were best learned in the German way, and who could consume the most alcohol. The men held court in the kitchen, and never with pride. There was never any physical outlet, sports activities etc, everyone just sat around drinking and belittling the world. To Diana those visits were such a putdown they subjected themselves to. Their own kids would never be as good as their friend's kids, and everyone would treat her like she was extremely naïve and handicapped because of her convent history. That was fair game. To add insult to injury – her husband wouldn't miss a chance to embarrass her in public.

He loved to talk; there was no stopping him. People would get up and leave and he would still be talking. He wouldn't take any hints from anyone, especially from her. That gave him reason to really humiliate and destroy her. He needed to prove his dominance every chance he had. Then he would gloat about her defeat. There was nothing sacred. Everyone needed to know their life history. She often wanted to crawl into a mouse hole. She felt extremely violated, especially since she had such a strong commitment to protect their privacy. There was not one time they got together with his German friends, that the guys didn't get drunk. The German Clubs, the Octoberfest, beer, and beer and bratwurst and sauerkraut and the German band were every year a much dreaded experience for her. At the end of every outing there was the ride home. Her erratic, drunk husband would insist on driving. They were almost killed several times. This stubborn, strong-willed behavior is not necessarily a bad attribute, but combined with alcohol abuse it gives every German a bad name.

At that time Diana used to wish that she wasn't German. She wanted to lose her German accent in the worst way, letting people mistake her for being Irish, without correcting. She wanted to be anything but German! As sad as it was, she could not carry the imprint of her heritage with pride.

Diana was trying to be acceptable to this country. This country's freedoms were new to her. She was so thankful for all the small favors. She remembered how surprised she was that people treated her so nice when she was pregnant. No funny looks or comments. She could go out; people would even smile at her; someone would open a door for her once or twice. She could even wear shorts or a swimsuit at the beach. Unbelievable! No one would have done that where she came from! A pregnant woman didn't show herself if at all possible, she'd stay put, "homebound", and hid it as long as she could. At least she'd wear some concealing clothing – as ugly as it was. Pregnancy was considered very private, or nothing to be flaunting, or be so proud of… What freedom in this country! What a life, what a relief!

She wanted to fit in. She wanted her children to be accepted, and have all the opportunities every other child had in this great country. She wanted them to have choices. She was trying to overcome what she perceived as an inadequacy and handicap. It was hard to be a foreigner. Any foreigner will agree with that. Any foreigner "by choice" has to have a strong desire for a better life, a desperate hope for a new chance. Even if one knew the language and customs of the new country, it was hard to survive without a support system of any family or friends. One had to earn respect and trust from the ground up, because no one knew you, or cared. You were on your own! In Diana's case, she thought it was fate that she ended up in the U.S.A. She wanted a new life. She thanked God for this new chance, and she was not afraid of working hard for it. She never gave herself any credit for overcoming the odds and hurdles of a foreigner. She worked from the first week she came to this country, with a few breaks in between when she had her children. She tried to do the best job. She frantically wanted to perfect her English, her Nursing techniques, learn all the new customs and move forward. She wanted to be an American. Most of all, she did not want to be German. She wanted to overcome this terrible stigma. It was not easy; she would get reminded of it over and over.

As time went on Diana felt the awesome weight of the wrongs that rested on German shoulders forever. She would never watch war movies or read Nazi history to this day. She will never watch "Schindler's List". Not that this would make a difference to anyone, or erase anything, but she was still trying to forget her own nightmares…

Diana wanted to file for her American Citizenship. That would finalize her decision to stay in the U.S.A., ground her, give her roots…Her children were born here, they were American citizens; she almost envied them. Her husband considered her a traitor. He was always going to be German. Really, she realized, he was afraid that she might become too liberated and independent.

Diana was sure that even her family would not understand. She could never tell her brother that she had ever denied being German. He would have felt that she had disgraced them. As it was, he always acted as though she deserted them; she left her homeland that he so fervently honored. Diana didn't blame him. After seven years in Siberia he must have vowed never to leave his home – Germany – if he ever saw it again. Somehow she always felt that he never forgave her for leaving.

Years later it gave everyone the greatest pleasure to hear her speak in a perfect Bavarian dialect – even after many years.

Diana realized that they had a bond – her brother and her – that super-ceded the normal planes of understanding. It was much more, it was unconditional acceptance of whatever she wanted to be or do. As she grew older this bond became stronger, and she enjoyed this priceless comfort more that she could say. He was not a man of many words, her brother, especially words of an emotional nature, but she felt what words couldn't say anyway: a sense of approval, forgiveness, peace and brotherly protectiveness.

If only she could have felt this as a child!

She now had this bond with her sisters as well. Amazing, considering that she had lived so far away from them and so different a life (or was it because of it?). Growing up she never felt as though she could measure up to them, maybe because they were so much older. She knew now that they had never judged her. She learned this too late in her life.

During many years she was not as close with any of her family, at least she did not feel that closeness. She could not even write to them. She was living such a different life she felt they could have never understood. Then she was too proud to admit that her life wasn't what it seemed to be, and certainly not as happy as she had told them. She lied a lot in her letters to them.

Diana acknowledged that she never was very good at making apologies or admitting failure. She was too busy fighting to keep her head above water. She wasn't supposed to fail. She was supposed to be perfect. Everyone looked at her as the one that broke out of the norm and moved on. She couldn't let them down. She had to keep up a good front. She could not show weakness or waste any energy thinking about it. She couldn't fail. Admitting to failure would have been too stifling and not allowed her to move forward. She could not have them worry about her. She told herself that she had made those choices – right or wrong – they were her mistakes, and she had to live with them. All the time she was discounting the fact that she really never had choices, but was blown in the direction of someone else's choosing, and landed in places through forces stronger than her.

No one could change a thing for her now. She would have to do it herself. She would have to take control of her life. This absolute independence of hers – do or die – she didn't quite understand herself. Perhaps she didn't want to answer for so many mistakes? Or was it just the fear that no one was going to catch her when she fell? She knew later she could have counted on her family, she could have come to them. Why didn't she know that then? They would have understood.

What about her pride? This pride, a friend of hers, was also her worst enemy at times. It set standards and expectations she sometimes could not live up to, and she always ended up feeling ashamed and debilitated when she fell short. Sometimes she cursed her pride. It would have been easier to give it up. She had to hold on to it, she needed to hold her head up and move on. That was the only way she knew how to survive. She could not jeopardize her pride. There was this underlying note that kept ringing in her ears all her life, and demanded her to stand tall and fend for herself – especially at times of major crisis, and when she needed help the most: "You made your bed, you lie in it." She heard that often enough. This always showed her the way real quickly. It was forward. She would have never gone back to anything. She had to do it alone. She never would fall back on her family. She never wanted to disappoint them. "Don't bring us any shame" still rang in her ears. Later, much later, Diana believed that they would have been there with open arms…

She hoped that her children would come home if they ever got in trouble.

Diana could not believe that she was the only German descent that struggled with these issues. Why was it that so many people never visited their homeland again, keeping their lives so private and often took their obvious hurtful secrets to their graves without resolve, leaving their children wonder why they could never talk about them. Children of German parents often told her later that she seemed to be "just like their mother." Did they all feel like traitors, deserters of their birth country, looking for a better life? Was it guilt, lack of loyalty to their "Vaterland" that haunted them, or the weight of the standards of their heritage, never lifted in their minds? Were they forever prisoners of old times, of their heritage, of their own wars?

On their visit to Germany with her husband and their children, her marriage unraveled. She had every intention to keep their troubles secret. Her parents noticed that things were wrong in her family – they could not help seeing it – Diana could not hide it any longer. Her husband gave it all away in one of his drunken fits, and worse than even she could have imagined. It was like a volcano erupted in her life, unexpected at this time, and devastating.

Drunk, and beside himself, when he did not get the sympathy he expected after he told her family all his complaints about her, he threw one of the kids in the car at 3 A.M. to drive to his parent's house. The entire family could not stop him. An hour later he returned with vomit all over the car and a child scared half to death. Diana's mother and sister helped her clean up the car for the rest of the night. Trying to justify his point, he went from house to house of everyone at least in her family, to tell them just how bad she was, her life story. They all showed him the door. Her parents, her sisters' and brothers' families who had witnessed his drunken, irrational behavior begged her to stay in Germany with them. There were jobs for nurses; they would take care of her children – anything but go back with this man to a faraway country where they had no one to help them.

Diana saw her mother crying her heart out as she waved good-bye.

Diana could not stay. She knew that her life would have to change. She had not expected this to happen at that time. It hurt more to have her parents agonize over them now that they knew than that she was hiding the truth from them, and lying to them for years. It hurt more than going back and enduring their lot again.

She could not stay. Then her husband would stay, too. The in-laws, his stepmother that beat up her children in the few days they were staying there, would mean "jumping into another frying pan." She had to go back. Her life, especially her children's lives were here in the U.S.A. Their lives would have to be better, they deserved the chance, and they were American Citizens .She would not rob them of that.

Also she could not stand the pity of her family. Everyone was so disturbed. One just did not bring his problems home in her time, and it was not in her nature to ask for help or depend on someone else, especially her family. She had to be strong. She had to help herself. She had some pride left...

Her parents' tears however burned in her heart. How dare her husband hurt them like that, and dump all their problems on them! Diana was so angry with him. She would never forgive him for that. Eventually she directed that anger where she always did: at herself. She was going to change things for sure. This time she would make things right. Her religious parents encouraged her to file for divorce, even though the concept of it was totally against their religious and moral beliefs. In their time divorce was unheard of; a woman had no rights, abused or not.

Diana was ready to file as soon as they would return to the USA..

However, there was only her, herself, and she, – and three children - too small to leave alone while she worked. The youngest had to be nine years old, said the attorney, before she could leave her with the older children. There were no childcare facilities like there are now. She could not take a chance to have her children taken away. The thought of it scared her to death. She knew no one that could watch them or that she would have trusted with her children. A single mother was equal to an unfit mother.

Her husband would pack his bags – and then stop at the door and cry, and the kids felt sorry for him, and she felt sorry for him, and he was sorry again – and he stayed. They tried again, and for a while it would be a little better. She would hold her breath, waiting for the next time, always afraid that something would jump out at her at any time...

After they came back from Germany, and he "stayed again" – they both made a lot of effort to make it work. They worked on the house, finished the basement; she stained some windows and planted flowers. Even he was proud of their accomplishments and seemed to enjoy the praise he'd get from neighbors. He even built the kids a tree house that all the kids in the neighborhood enjoyed.

It reminded Diana of her cherry tree, her heaven, when she was a child. Somehow she hoped that this tree house was a "safe-haven" for her children, a place to be carefree as a child should be...

When they had company from his friends with their families, he'd take all the kids to the park, and the mothers would envy her, because they thought their husbands weren't half as nice. He enjoyed all their attention and praise, and especially making their husbands jealous. He could be charming in front of other people. They did not know that after they went home he'd continue to get drunk and beat up his kids at the drop of a hat.

He worked with his hands; they were huge and strong. Diana thought he was going to break their son's back once – holding him up in the air with one hand, and slapping him across his back with the other, over and over… When she threw herself against him pleading with him to stop, it only angered him more, and he threw all of them across the entire room, like Frisbees.

The baby would cry upstairs while he was working in the basement, and he would run upstairs and spank the baby. How could you stop a baby from crying by slapping her on her naked butt? He was sick. He had lost control. He was an alcoholic. However, he would never admit that he had a problem, and he would get very angry just at the suggestion. It was always she that had the problem because in the end she would break down and cry, and this weakness of hers would give him pleasure, it would give him power. He felt triumphant; he had won. She had no defense, no way out. She was just not strong enough. She believed it. Where was her pride anymore?

It became more and more difficult to keep their lives private, as she needed it to be, as her culture and upbringing demanded of her. She would actually protect him and justify his behavior. She would never acknowledge that he had a mental- and alcohol problem to anyone, and she would deny it to herself, because she was ashamed that she couldn't fix or at least handle it. She betrayed herself. Looking back, she knew she was kidding herself, everyone knew it. Some of her children's teachers would occasionally stop over at their house; they tried to help, she knew now. They would ask her about her husband, and if everything was OK. She made excuses for his volatile behavior. She would not admit any problems because she didn't want it to reflect on the children. She could handle the bruises, but the dark side, the mean streak in him, that became increasingly apparent, frightened her.

They went to church every Sunday. Actually her husband had become very "religious" in a warped sense – and it would be hell for the rest of the day. He had been at church and that would excuse everything.

The kids played the church organ. They were very talented. They won first place in all the organ and piano contests, even in the state competition. She was very proud of them. She knew he was proud of them, too. He enjoyed the kids when his anger and temper and alcohol didn't dominate him. When was that? When his sickness got the best of him, it was her fault, always. She drove him to it, something she did or didn't do, or say, or buy. Diana really believed it. She was so insecure after years of being beaten down she let every wind blow her over. She thought it must be her fault. She assumed his guilt and carried his baggage… Fighting became senseless and too hard, she didn't have the nerve to stand up to him anymore, she was afraid of his temper, and she was a coward. There was some comfort in the "constant", even if it was an abusive environment, she justified; it was still scary to break out of it.

There were three funerals in Germany within one year: her father's, her mother's and her brother's. She flew home to all of them, which severely stretched their budget. They were devastating experiences for her. She didn't need those losses at that time of her life, or at any time. There were many tears…

One Fourth of July weekend Diana was hemorrhaging so much that an emergency hysterectomy had to be scheduled for the following Monday. She didn't even question the doctor's decision. Actually she was somewhat relieved by the thought that she didn't have to worry about getting pregnant again. She thanked God for his providence in these events – another choice her conscience didn't have to bear.

She carried on, one day at a time, trying to cope, doing what she believed was her best, though it may not have been good enough or soon enough. Tomorrow it would change. She would get stronger. Someday she could stand on her own....

Diana would worry herself sick while at work, and call home constantly. Of course, no one at work knew any of her problems. She kept her secrets well. She often heard the kids crying in the background. When the children were grown, they would talk about it. They weren't allowed to tell her what was going on, that their father came home drunk again and beat them up again. If she had known everything that went on at home, she couldn't have handled it and their marriage would have been over long before it was. She blamed herself enough for being away. Her husband blamed everything on her having a job. They really couldn't feed a family of five on his salary, nor could they live in the "hole that was enough for him." This meant that he was happy and content, and she had too many ambitions and was "never satisfied." That was a sin. What about a future for their children? What about a college education?

Then he was going to change again, and he was sorry, and they tried again for another year.

There were some highlights again: There was Christmas! Diana bought the kids lots of presents every year, trying to make up for everything else... trying to make up for the presents and attention they never received from relatives and everyone else... trying to recreate the warm Christmas she remembered from her simple, poor, cold childhood home... She exhausted herself every year to make it a happy time, a spiritual time with carols, plays, peace...

She wondered later why for many years after she felt so vulnerable at Christmas time, why she burst into tears so easily while trimming the tree... every year. Were the memories catching up with her of the heightened despair and conflict that became most apparent every year at holiday time... the memories she denied and never wanted to feel again?

Then there were piano-and organ concerts and contests of the children, a vacation in California and Colorado, where her husband was a different person, probably without the alcohol... Diana wanted to move there, but she realized that their problems would move with them.

They tried to move away from the old neighborhood, the taverns where her husband would routinely stop on his way home from work in the afternoon, or go back to with the kids later. They would start new; they built a new house with no memories, but it was cold and empty. Somehow he became more possessive and controlling than ever. The lady across the street invited her in to see her new house one time. Her husband came home from work; he rang every doorbell in the neighborhood, looking for her. When he found her he was at his belligerent best. Then he called her neighbor every five minutes until she went home. She was embarrassed to death, and made the usual excuses for him, but she saw her last hope for a new start dwindling fast.

Somehow she had to muster up the courage to move forward, one day at a time. Only forward wasn't the way to go. Diana saw the fork in the road, and it became clearer and clearer that the direction had to change. She didn't' want to have to make this choice. Marriage was a sacred commitment. Somehow divorce seemed the "lesser evil".

She stained a big window in their den with her own creation of "you are the architect of your life". She didn't know what made her paint it. It was beautiful. Only it reminded her every day that this concept wasn't for her. She wasn't free. Would her children ever be free?

This window troubled her; it stirred up her soul. It stared her in the face every day. Did she have a choice?

Even in their new house there was no love; it didn't matter where they lived.

She remembered envying people that showed love and affection and kindness toward each other, even in public, something they were never destined to have.

At one point she signed up for ballroom dancing lessons at a studio, thinking that maybe if she learned how to dance they could achieve some sense of closeness. They went a couple of times. It was no use. It was such a sham.

Diana's job was the only thing she had that her husband could not control. Someday it would allow her to break out of this vise and support them. Sometimes she'd take the kids to work to visit her, and they could not believe that she was actually someone. She was a whole different person at work than the mouse at home. People actually respected her; they even looked up to her and liked her... She was a great nurse. She could patch up everyone's wounds and solve everyone's problems except her own. She could hide behind the uniform, always fine, with not a problem of her own. She could only cry on her way to and from work. Work was her therapy as well, at least she could forget about her life for a little while. She could have thought of a hundred things she would have had aptitude or talents for, or would have preferred to do other than nursing. She had long given up hope for other choices and aspirations in her life. Her spirit was chained to reality. She thanked God for her job every day; it was stability. This job put bread on the table. There was good health insurance. They needed it. Her heart was acting up, she had several surgeries and a ruptured disc that severely limited her for years, not to mention the constant pain…There were enormous dental problems with all the children. Their father had dentures in his twenties. They needed that health insurance. She was afraid to miss a day of work because she was scared to death of losing her job. She needed that job, that security, if she ever could give them a better life.

There were no support groups or shelters for abused families that she knew of. They had no place to go. She could never talk to anyone about her private life; no wonder most people were shocked when they divorced. The people they knew thought they had the perfect marriage. So, she would swallow, and swallow, and go on – one day at a time, one boot at a time, waiting for tomorrow to show her the way out, and hoping that it would hurt a little less tomorrow…

Once in a while she would run away in her despair, though she knew of no one to run to, and no one that could help. She wanted to find a place that could swallow her up. There was no place. There was no cherry tree… She had been at the church, and the priests would patronizingly pat her on the back and tell her to be strong and go home to her husband. Marriage was a sacrament – "until death do us part". Divorce was not popular; everyone had enough of his or her own problems. So when she would "runaway", she would drive to an empty parking lot and cry for a few hours. Of course she had to go back home, the children were home…

Her husband would laugh at her when she walked in the door, because he also knew that she had no place to go…

Diana hated him when he would then walk around the house whistling and singing at the times of her worst despair. She remembered locking herself in the bathroom, and running a bath forever, so she wouldn't hear it anymore. Afterwards she cried herself to sleep, too many times...How could she have thought that the children were not aware of this?

Their marriage was over long before the divorce was final. She had to rescue herself as well as her children before they all sank. The abuse was also crippling the children, and it was time to salvage what was left. She wouldn't tell them not to respect their father, so she swept everything under the mat, pretending...She said nothing. She hated discord – in music as much as in the atmosphere. She did whatever necessary to end it. She had to find a way to make things seem ok. Sometimes they didn't talk for weeks. You could have cut the silence. God knows why she thought it was better than fighting. She lived in denial for a long time. She knew better. She betrayed her children and herself.

One day while driving home from a shopping trip her fourteen-year-old daughter asked her why they were staying together. It shocked her. She didn't want to believe that the children knew how bad it was. She learned that they were more aware than she realized. They understood other families were different than theirs. They had started to feel undeserving of a better life, a family life that she wanted for them.

The attorney that handled her divorce knew she was barely hanging on...She remembered crying incessantly throughout every meeting and being so embarrassed... He was very fatherly, and tried to protect her interests, as well as the children's.

It wasn't over when Diana thought it was. Her husband didn't think there was anything wrong, and he was not going to allow her to get a divorce. He owned her. She could not do anything without his permission. He would stalk her everywhere. He'd sit across the street from her work in his car, waiting 'til she drove out at midnight – and follow her. She was so scared to drive home for some time, never knowing whether he was behind her, or if he was waiting around the next corner, or at the house. He was there, everywhere. She never knew what he might do. She was afraid of him. She had nowhere to go.

Diana will never forget the twenty-mile drive on the expressway one day during their separation - with him on her bumper, and the kids screaming in the car, which was after he grabbed the youngest and her friend out of her car at the last stop. His face in the rearview mirror was that of a very sick person. He was mean and calculating, and didn't care what happened to them at that point. He had lost control. After she dropped off her daughter's little friend at her house (her parents never spoke to her again), it was another twenty miles back home – with him on her bumper at 55 miles an hour. She couldn't even be sure at what speed she drove. Finally she lost him at the red light just before their house, and she locked all the doors when they arrived home. After he threatened to break all the windows, and had the entire neighborhood in front of their house, screaming – the police finally arrived and convinced him to leave. This time at least.

It was inconceivable for him that she could separate herself from him, he owned her for life; she was his property. He relished sympathy from everyone they knew, neighbors, church, friends or strangers. He was a martyr all his life. He liked that role. Diana was tired. She didn't want to justify their divorce to anyone. She didn't care if she was the villain or not. She was too battered and exhausted. She just needed to survive.

All of those years Diana had lied in her letters home to her family. Like anyone believed a word she said!

Diana only wished that their visit to Germany had not been the last time her parents saw her children, and that they could at least have died thinking that they were OK. She would have lied for the rest of her life to give them that peace, but when they died, she didn't have to pretend any longer. She liked to think that her parents were somewhere in her corner, around them - still, a comforting feeling. She often asked them for their advice and help, and especially to watch over their grandchildren, and their children someday.

The effects of that chapter of her life were most destructive. Diana wondered what traumas her children carried away from their childhood... They never talked about it. It *hurt too much.*

They survived, and she was proud to see in her children integrity, honor, pride and kindness, the values, the "royal blood" of her heritage. She saw in them strength to move forward despite obstacles, never giving up, and being true. She hoped that they knew that they had many choices, and that their spirit would always be free.

However, reading this chapter twenty years later, as Diana decided to publish this book, she found herself crying throughout.

VIII

ROYAL   BLOOD

Diana was divorced… Scary. Another turn in her life! Someone said "there are no mistakes in life, only opportunities to perfect ones purpose in this world." She thought this was so kind. However she felt like a bag of broken glass. Now it was just picking up the pieces once more, and going on. Once more stranded – but on her feet still. There were no tears. Her parents would have been proud, she thought. There was no time to waste. She had to be strong. She had three children.

Somehow she felt liberated when it was over. She was on a mission to free her spirit. They changed their name, her and the kids. It was an act of emancipation and freedom, the appearance at least that she could stand on her own. Anything to pull them up. Why not change the name back? Her maiden name was German and hard to pronounce. At this point she thought she wanted to cut all strings, all loyalties to everything. Perhaps she couldn't handle the guilt of disgracing her family. Anyway - they picked a name out of the phonebook.

Diana remembered stopping for lunch in a restaurant on the way to work one day, right after her divorce. She had to force herself to overcome the fear of standing alone. She was so insecure that she swore everyone was staring at her and could see her torn soul. She couldn't eat her meal.

Years later, while out to breakfast with her children at a local restaurant, she rejected a cold meal. She had never asserted herself before. Her children were shocked and embarrassed. They were not used to this, and not one of them could assert themselves either. They would have long eaten the food cold.

They would have to change that. They would have to learn to say "no".

Her job was the only security she had; she could not lose it. She didn't know how she held together, but somehow she never missed a day of work.

Her daughter once asked her, why she put herself through the ordeal of getting an annulment from the church? She herself wondered, why. Was it that she had to overcome the haunting religious fears that were instilled in her all her life from childhood on, not to mention in the convent…?

She remembered hanging up the phone on her parish priest after her ex-husband told him about their divorce. Without any question he scolded and threatened her with everything including hell. If she did not repent and take her husband back, she would be an outcast from the church excluded from all sacraments, etc. Diana hung up on him; she could not handle this.

How did he that Priest know what her hell was? She didn't have the strength to argue or explain to anyone anymore. No one could possibly know or understand. Now she was rejected from the "authority" of the church, her church that she had committed her life to. What was there left? She wondered if God rejected her, too. Where was her loving God? Was she being punished for failing? Failing again? This fear weighed heavily on her. The German word "angst" describes the feeling better. It has the meaning of a crushing, disabling, consuming fear…and "angst"-ridden she was.

Diana felt that day like this priest had closed the door on her. She didn't go to church anymore. After she caught her balance a little, she still was seeking some approval from the church. She couldn't lose her church, her faith...Perhaps she was looking for some closure. She wasn't trying to justify her divorce – but she thought, surely someone would have to understand, and not condemn her all together. She remembered sitting through sessions and confessions at the parish and the Archdiocese, crying like a mindless child – so devastated that any idiot should have seen that this divorce was her last resort. She was barely clinging on to a thread of sanity before she would crash. That crash seemed imminent and inevitable. She often wondered if these priests had ever seen such a basket case. This entire process was very intimidating, and the priests were no help. She received no solace or refuge from the church. She walked away from this ashamed and destroyed.

The marriage was annulled.

She never did understand it. It never made much sense to her. So the marriage was nullified, like it never happened? Believe her, it did.

She had three children, the only blessings from her marriage. It happened. So, now could she go to church again, of course without receiving any sacraments? Everything was well again? She was not rejected anymore? She was still divorced.

A couple of years later Diana attended a funeral mass of a neighbor. The priests walked through the aisles, distributing communion to everyone, including her husband who wasn't even catholic. Diana bowed her head. She was divorced. It still hurt.

She was not sure anyone would understand her problem. She was taught that to be unworthy of receiving communion was a greater sin than not to receive it at all. The question was in her mind: Who ever thought he was worthy at all?

She wrote to the missionary priest that brought her to the convent school when she was fourteen. Sometimes after she had left the convent she heard that he had told her superiors there that "they had ruined a beautiful child." She always trusted that he knew her, the real her, her soul. She thought he would know that she always tried her best, even if she failed. He knew she was married, and used to write to her sometimes. However, when she told him that her marriage failed after fifteen years, he chastised and deserted her, too. She was totally crushed after she read his last letter, and never wrote to him again. She sure could have used some understanding, someone in her court...

Diana had never felt so alone. She had to bury the hurt really deep....

She called on two of their previous parish priests for help, not for her, but to talk to her children at least, to help them cope with the divorce and their troubles. The priests knew her children well, they had gone to that Catholic school and church for years, played the church organ, received their sacraments there, her son was an altar boy...Perhaps they would help?

Without the desperately needed help from her church and all the people she had loved and respected – she found her balance in her own soul again. She had not lost her faith. God was still there. She could still pray. She found her own way. It was the church, not God that had rejected her. God is good...

Diana told this to her thirteen-year-old son when he found out that he was rejected from taking his Confirmation just a few days before the big day. He wasn't ready, the pastor told him, he didn't behave well enough, and he didn't deserve it… She heard her son tell the pastor that he hoped God didn't feel the same way about him…It was a vulnerable and lonesome time for them. She almost had given up the hope that a superior being had more plans for her.

Sometimes she felt like she had lived several different lives – and died a few deaths. Her daughter kept asking her: "What carried you through it all?" What allowed her to emerge from one disaster after another, and even stronger every time? If she had to sum it up, she would have to attribute it to her free spirited soul, a strong "life force", that nothing could quite destroy, a rebellious trait that always forced her to break out of, to defy, to overcome, to fight and never give up. Yes, her pride… where was her pride? It would surface again; it always did. Were there a few drops of royal blood in her veins left from her ancestors?

Somehow she never liked to see herself as a victim, but a survivor. She never believed in fate, she always thought one could at least influence ones destiny. She worked hard at fighting for survival, fighting for her soul and her identity, fighting the fears and demons of her life. To survive was the strongest family trait she inherited. Perhaps she kept fighting because she didn't have a choice. She always thought she had to make the best of a situation, to "make it work". She never knew that she had a choice to stay or leave without shame …

Diana had learned now that life didn't need to be so full of hardships. One can make choices at every instant, every day.

Life would have to be better from then on. It was. Not that there was no turbulence from then on, like raising three teenager. They had their own troubles. She wished she could have healed their wounds, and filled all their voids. She also wished she could give them their childhood back without scars and abuse, and been the perfect mother she could have been. She felt quite at a loss at that time. What happened to her ideals of a beautiful family, a better life for her children? Someday, someday…

She wished she had taught them to climb cherry trees…

Diana didn't think they would ever know how hard she tried to make a warm and peaceful home for them as well as be mother and father and provider. They were growing up and away too fast, and it seemed that she could never give enough.

She certainly had no time or energy for self-pity. Her ex-husband had gone from house to house in their entire neighborhood gathering sympathy and pity for himself. She didn't have time or any intentions to defend or explain her side, or announce her tragedies to the entire world. As it was, she was desperately trying to hold on to a little dignity. The police had been at their house when he was going to smash all the windows. The children were embarrassed and slowly became alienated from their friends. They could never repair the damage. Her ex-husband had still not accepted the divorce and would never give them any peace.

Diana's place of work was 25 miles away. She needed to be close to home. They had to move. She found a house – five minutes from work, thank God; she would have to run home often enough. She bought the house with every penny of her portion of the divorce settlement. She had no money for movers. So she loaded up her car, and unloaded it on her way to work, every day for weeks. They only needed a friends' truck and help for moving a few large pieces of furnishings. The basement of the old house she had bought was flooded with a foot of sewer-water when they moved in, and some friends from work fixed the sump pump. The wet carpet weighed a ton, and she had to cut it up in small squares to be able to carry them out.

The total responsibility for the children, a roof over their head, new schools, new neighborhood, everything was hers, and it weighed heavily on her. She felt the eyes of her new neighbors watching her with skepticism. Was preserving her privacy really worth the price to pay? She had never had friendly neighbors. Now that she thought of it, neither did her parents. She never thought she had any skills to make friends. She had no time to go over for coffee or a barbeque etc. to neighbors, she was too private a person to share. There was Pat, Diana swore she was a true friend, however after her divorce she never heard from her again. Diana felt like she lived in a world all by herself, just as she did as a child. And the same loss of friends, of people around her, haunted her throughout her life.

Why was she surprised that she would find herself standing in the shadows of her childhood, the war times, when "you couldn't trust your brother", when you had to hide and bury everything that was dear to you, or loose it? Diana saw the distrust and caution in her mother's eyes, looking someone over… Her instincts that would tell her that it was better not to have friends than keeping the wrong company. Her father's words still echoed in her ears: "You can't trust anyone until you have eaten a sack of salt with him." She cringed when she thought of her parents' most desperate times when "neighbors were too greedy to share", and relatives "didn't care if their children died of hunger". Why would she be surprised to find herself standing in these shadows? Why was she still fighting these battles today?

It seemed that the war machine was still running…and still casting its shadow…

Bearing the sole responsibility for her family now wasn't really different, but she was physically and mentally exhausted and ended up in the hospital again with heart problems. There were many long nights when she couldn't sleep because she was scared of the next day. In the daylight, however, she dared the world to try to cheat her out of her right to survive. Her pride slowly surfaced again. She was relentlessly stubborn and determined to pull herself up. When she became discouraged and depressed, she would throw herself into some kind of project that demanded her full attention for the moment, until she was able to handle her life again. She fixed and painted the entire house by herself, because she couldn't afford any help.

On the weekends the kids would help tear and drag out the old carpeting of the rest of the house, clean and paint and they slept on the floor exhausted. With the children's bank account that she had saved for them (the only money they had to their name), they found a wholesale company to carpet their entire house. When they were done, it was a nice house. Friends from work even helped them build a pool later, and when the furnace went out in the middle of winter, they would work all night at her house rebuilding the motor, sometimes on company time. She had friends now! She was so grateful for so much of their support and help during that time, and she was grateful to the company and her bosses. She never knew she had such good friends.

There were challenges, new schools and difficulties with being accepted as a divorcee with three children in an all-Italian neighborhood, children's cars, friends and struggles. She was completely broke, but she knew that she would pull out of it. She worked seven days a week that first year, either at her job or at an area hospital on her days off. She paid two mortgages until the old house finally sold a year later. Much rather she would have stayed home, and enjoyed her children and their new home. She could only dream of that. This was all she could handle at the time. Her ex-husband was no help with anything, but gave her a lot of grief. She had to borrow money from friends to close on the house, to fix the driveway, the garage door, the roof, electrical work…She always managed to pay it right back, and keep going, and going. She knew that they would survive. It was up to her, and there was nothing she would not do, or could not do.

Diana started to enjoy her freedom, the freedom to make her own choices! What a precious gift! She could be herself – not that she exactly knew who that was. She knew she was OK. Slowly she regained some confidence and felt emotionally stronger. Now she would have to try to fit in with the rest of the world. She had her hair cut short, and she colored it lighter.

She put rollers in her hair. Her ex-husband would have disapproved of such "vanity". She remembered driving to work that day dreading the reaction. To her surprise and initial embarrassment, everyone loved it. From then on she would curl her hair, look in the mirror, sometimes she would even wear lipstick. She'd dress more attractive and she traded her glasses for contact lenses. One day she even shaved her legs, which was a first. She would sing in the car driving to and from work, enjoying her freedom as well as trying to work up courage to face the world another day.

She learned to smile again. On Friday nights she would go out with the girls after work for a drink, or for pizza, a birthday or a Christmas party, something she was never allowed to do. She always had to be home from work precisely when her ex-husband expected her. Sometimes everyone danced at the lounge to some songs on the jukebox. She would watch them with envy and politely decline an invitation to join. No one would believe that she couldn't dance. People she worked with and knew her for many years noticed the transformation. They'd tell her she was a different person. They seemed to enjoy her coming out of her shell, and she was the subject of many harmless jokes. It felt good to be "one of them", and they treated her like their younger sister.

She allowed herself to open up and get a little closer to people. It was time to overcome the distrust and fear of betrayal she carried around with her for too long. She even invited a few people to her house and became friends with them, a few Caucasian people, African American people, Kim Kim, her Korean friend. Very cautiously she let her hair down and shared a problem or two with a co-worker, which she had never ever done.

Diana was terribly reluctant and afraid of leaving herself open to other's perceptions, opinions and judgment. She had kept too many secrets too long. Why were the opinions of others so important to her? Was privacy the only safe way to preserve her honor? Perhaps she couldn't leave what little she had to chance. Her honor was all she had, without that she had nothing, as her father always said. Perhaps someone would discover that she wasn't perfect after all? It was a trade-off: her vulnerability for the freedom and courage to accept who she was.

What a change! People opened up to her because she was not only the nurse and counselor for their problems, but had some of her own. She became one of them. They invited her into their lives. She felt connected. She'd listen to her colored friends' locker room stories with new ears, their hopes of breaking out of their crime-ridden, unsafe neighborhoods, their stories of abuse and their fears for their children.

Their struggles with issues of discrimination and intimidation, their fight for survival and freedom, their hopes for a better life were not so different from hers. She could identify with their issues – not of color or race – but of poverty and suppression and limited choices, the cultural stigmas of her heritage.

So she became human at last. At last she accepted the liberating fact that it was OK to be less than perfect, that it was OK to be whoever she was. It felt wonderful. It felt like breaking chains…How many layers of bondage would she have to break to ever be free?

In that environment Diana found her new husband-to-be. She wasn't looking for a husband. She didn't "need" a partner. She suddenly had many guy-friends as well as girlfriends and she valued their friendships. There were opportunities for relationships, and guys would ask her out. She started to feel valued and deserving. This was a first in her life. She had never looked at another man, and would not allow herself an unfaithful thought until the end of her marriage. This was a whole new experience for her. Some married men would approach her, and she learned that there were other kinds of bad marriages. She was busy, spending time with her children, making a home, fixing the house in her spare time, besides working six or seven days. She really didn't think she had that much to attract a man, other than her very bare and hard-working self.

Yet there he was. There was something about him that no one else had.

For the first time in her life Diana knew what attraction felt like. It wasn't hard to fall in love with him. He was an intelligent man; he was sincere and kind. He had much the same values as she did, hard-working, devoted to his job, had worked for the same company for many years, and was now Manager of the evening shift she also worked. He was never married, had no children and was about her age. She admired that he never had a bad thing to say about anyone, which was unusual in an environment where there was much competitiveness and back-stabbing going on especially in his ranks of the company. Another honorable quality she liked in him was his kindness to his elderly parents. He would visit them almost every weekend and take his dad on several fishing trips every year. When he moved to a new apartment, she offered to help with moving, hanging drapes, and a few cosmetic things, and he was excited and grateful. He thought she was talented and smart.

However, he had a girlfriend he had been seeing on and off for years. For the first time Diana felt jealousy, and she felt like she deserved better. She wanted a whole relationship or nothing. He broke off the relationship with that girl. Diana started going out for pizza after work with him, and sometimes she would wait for him for an hour, because he always worked late. This she didn't mind. He listened to all her work-and other troubles. She could be herself with him, without any inhibitions or secrets…She could cry all the tears saved up for a lifetime and he still liked and respected her.

They kept their relationship private, because the company really didn't approve of hourly employees dating a manager. No sweat; she was an expert at that. They went to Las Vegas, one of his favorite vacation spots, which gave them some private time to get to know each other. This was where they were married a year later.

Her new husband treated her wonderfully. He wouldn't dream of embarrassing her in public; he had excellent manners, dressed well and never was loud or inappropriate. To top it all, he was very handsome. He took care of himself. Diana looked up to him. She was proud to be in his company. He'd pick up the tab and she didn't "owe" him. He'd never have five drinks too many. If she ever wanted anything, he'd say, "You should have it." It was so nice to be spoiled.

He was a big man with a big voice. Because of this, it took a while for her to trust that he was not mean, and for a long time she was startled whenever he would speak.

She came to love his parents like her own. His mother "adopted" her entire family. She never forgot her children's birthdays, and treated them like her own grandchildren.

It seemed like everything was looking up. Diana's husband was very protective of her children. They respected his opinion, his patience, intelligence and tactfulness. . He was fair and kind, and there was no more abuse. He wanted her to quit working and spend time at home. They could afford to live on his salary. She respected him for stepping in and helping in the support of the children. He was incredibly generous. For some odd reason she convinced him to let her work a little longer, to save some money of her own, to save money for her children's education, or to give them a good start in life.

Was this too good to be true?

They remodeled the house with new windows, a new kitchen, a patio door and a beautiful deck. Her husband enjoyed the same things she did. He was proud of their projects and accomplishments as much as she was. He loved her talents. One day the entire family helped together removing all the old awnings over the windows. They sprayed them dark brown with a white trim, and the kids were climbing like monkeys on the house screwing them back on – all in the same day. When their neighbors came home from work they didn't recognize their house. Another new emotion… She was proud.

The first six-months of their marriage they were able to save a down payment for a six-flat apartment building which her daughter and she bought, their first dabbling in real estate. It was a successful venture. Her daughter built herself an apartment in the basement to live in for a few years after her marriage, and it sold later for a good profit.

Diana became an American Citizen. At last she belonged. Independence, liberty, justice, freedom – it sounded fine to her! She was proud to stand on her own two feet. It felt like success. She had earned it.

IX

BREAKING   THE   CHAIN

Their new marriage had barely started when Diana's new husband lost his job. Life is not kind. This relationship was different. They were partners. She thought she could conquer the world with him by her side. She thought she was strong. They thought they would work together on whatever the future would bring. Of course, it would be a fight for survival again for the next years to come. What else was new in her life?

Her husband was fired. No reason. It was inconceivable for her husband to be "fired". He had the perfect work record, never took a sick day in more than twenty-one years, worked ten to twelve hour days and was loyal and dedicated to the company. The shift he managed consistently had the best production record of the three shifts. Only he did not know that the new young personnel manager had the "mission" to get rid of the older middle management. There were other men and women like him that had invested their lives in this great private company. Some of them were already gone. They blamed themselves for incompetence, for their own failure to "adapt to the new changes" in the company. It ruined their lives. Some lost their families. They certainly lost most of their retirement from the company that was promised to them. They found out later that theirs wasn't the only company that found ways to cut their workforce. It became a trend that the older or sickly people should go.

They had a vacation scheduled in Las Vegas the weekend after her husband was fired. They went anyway. At the check-in counter of the hotel he gave them his ID, and when he was asked where he worked – he froze. He just stood there – white like a sheet. That's when it hit him. He said: "My God, I don't have a job." Diana thought he was going to have a heart attack. For her husband his job was his identity. There was integrity in having a job. He had worked all his life. He was ashamed to his core.

Diana really started to worry about him. He was a stable man. He was honest and sincere. He had always planned things well. He had invested his life in this company for a reason. Growing up poor, he had vowed that he would plan his life to be better off some day than his poor struggling parents. The loss of his job was like a death; it took away his life's purpose. He had loved his job; he was married to this company. It was incomprehensible for him to have lost his job.

The other two managers that worked alongside him in the same positions were much younger. They were not fired. Years ago no one thought of age discrimination. In time, it was noticeable at their company that while the younger people survived and new young people were hired replacing older workers, the older population shrunk.

Her husband was in shock, and became more depressed by the day. The kids had come to know him and care about him. When they would find him alone in the house in the dark in the middle of the day...they were scared for him.

She worked for the same company as an industrial nurse. The same supervisor that fired her husband asked her a couple of times if she was still "going out" with her "boyfriend". No one knew they were married. She told her that she better know where her loyalties are. That day Diana decided to fight. She realized that she was a target, too.

Diana thought she was jinxed, she was done All she wanted was peace. Once more she had gathered up all her strength and courage to go forward –she could not bear to have anyone take it away. Besides this was all wrong. For once in her life, her loyalties were going to be in the right place. Fear and intimidation – even though they were nagging at her – were not going to get the best of her this time. To this day she had always respected her bosses at work. She never said "no", she did a perfect job (so did her husband), she followed the rules, and look where it got them! Again up against authority – of the job, her boss, the beloved company, the justice system. The authority of this great country, the law, was this time going to set things straight, she prayed, and for once in her life come around to help and heal and validate instead of intimidate and punish. Of course she summoned God and all Saints and Angels and her parents and friends in heaven to help. It was easier for her *to* fight for someone else than for herself. She had more courage as they deserved better. Certainly her husband deserved better. She was always fighting for the underdog, just never for herself.

At least the company did not know that they were married. No one did for years. They knew better than to tell – she would be fired next. Diana was the breadwinner now, again. This was the best kept secret at the company ever, they said, when they found out much later, which was very unusual for their company rumor mill.

The day after this supervisor threatened her job she convinced her husband that they had to fight this. They just couldn't lie down and die. He was not a fighting man, her husband, and it took a lot of convincing. He would always diffuse and mediate acute situations at his job in a calm, controlled, fair manner. There was always a way to work things out reasonably. He cared about the people he managed. People would come up to her and tell her how fair and patient he was, how he had helped them get better training and pay and advancements at their jobs. Everyone respected him. Perhaps it would be good for him to talk to his supervisors that knew him for many years, to find out what happened. He tried. No one wanted to get involved. Everyone was concerned to keep his or her own job. No one could give him an explanation or a reason. There were several meetings. He wasn't allowed to come into the building anymore. He was treated like a nuisance. He wrote a letter to the owner of the company. It was turned over to the person that fired him in the first place to resolve. Nothing was resolved. Over the next several weeks he tried to negotiate. He wasn't given any alternatives. He wasn't given a choice in the matter. He was still fired.

Her husband felt like his life was over. The fact that he was fired without a reason only made the situation worse. He was just discarded like he never had any value. It didn't matter to anyone whether he was there or not, or had done a good job or not. It took away his dignity.

They went to see an attorney. He was very interested at first. Later they found out that the company paid him off. The E.E.O.C. (Equal Employment Opportunity Commission) was next. It was the same there. The person that had done an investigation, and did her job, was promoted out of that office. Dead again.

Then a factory mechanic who was ailing with throat cancer, came into Diana's office one day and slammed his fist on her desk, saying: "It was wrong, what they did." He left an attorney's card on her desk. They went to see that attorney, who actually filed a lawsuit.

That attorney believed in their case. He started to take depositions, and then suddenly left the law firm and disappeared. The Bar Association said that he was no longer practicing law. When they refused to give up, the firm referred them to a trial attorney, which was the best thing that could have happened to them.

Her husband had since calculated that his retirement income had shrunk by ten-times, since now he would be in a vested vs. a working retirement plan when he was fifty. They knew now what the reason was for getting people out before they were fifty.

Everyone at the company laughed at them, at least initially. The management would tell her that there was no way they would win a lawsuit against the company. Who did they think they were? It could not be done. No one took them seriously.

What kind of an idiot would think of taking on a Fortune 500 Company? Age Discrimination?

No one actually said: "You are fired because you are too old". No one had blatantly spelled it out. They all had loved this company. It was a privately owned company. They all felt part of it. No one could believe that they would cut someone's throat. Diana remembered some years before, when the company would stretch someone $10,000.00 so he wouldn't lose his house. A young woman was quietly put back on her mother's health insurance (that she was no longer entitled to at 26 years of age), because she was diagnosed with terminal cancer. Diana worked with workers' compensation cases and people on sick leave, and the company treated them with compassion and kindness. They bailed an employee out of jail once or twice. The company used to have a heart. It was a family.

They had company picnics and dinner dances and sports events, etc. No one in his right mind would believe that this same company would play dirty. The employees were totally loyal. It was an unwritten contract that if you worked hard and did a good job, the company would take care of you when you were old with a good retirement.

The company took on a new face. There were changes in management and a change in company philosophy, a "generational" change. It was a slow, well covered-up process. The bottom line became profit. The emphasis shifted from the value of keeping dedicated, long-term employees to saving more money. Someone figured out that the company could save millions if the older, higher-paid employees retired early.

Many times, Diana and her husband would go for months without hearing from the attorney. They lost faith many times. It was a struggle to keep pushing on.

The environment at the company became hostile and threatening for Diana. Her job was not secure, to say the least, and she received many subtle threats.

She had to watch every step she made. After almost 20 years of documented outstanding performance reviews she – all of a sudden – could not do anything right. People were set up to watch her every move. It felt like the convent. They had subliminal tapes, "bugs" and cameras everywhere. They didn't imagine this; the information came from their national office. Diana's entire job was turned upside down, her hours changed constantly. She had a new supervisor every couple of months. She was given erratic assignments that were in no way related to her job. Censured and harassed on a daily basis, she dreaded to go to work.

However, she not only needed that job, she had to do a perfect job. Even worse than the threat of losing her job, was the fear of them trying to professionally discredit her. It was hard enough to be a patient advocate as a nurse, while the company paid her salary. Now that tension was accelerated. Confidentiality of records was a continuous battle. She refused to jeopardize her professional ethics.

Diana could never stand to see people hurt or treated unfairly. It went against her grain, her principles. She had no choice but to fight for them. She remembered at one occasion being requested to turn records of all employees that had any handicaps or disabilities of any kind over to the personnel manager, who was her boss as well as the person that fired her husband. She refused, and after an ultimatum – she cut all the names off the printouts before she turned them over. She told her manager that if she wanted it for statistical purposes only, she didn't need the names. She was surprised that she didn't fire her for her total defiance. However, she was not the only R.N. there. Incidentally, none of the workers on the "list with no names" survived the year at the company. They all were either let go, or put on early retirement or long-term disability leaves of which they never returned. The handwriting was on the wall; some of the employees were catching on. It became apparent that the older employees were treated differently, challenged with new technology jobs they couldn't learn anymore - it was suggested. They were told that they were inflexible and opposed to change. Most were embarrassed and scared off, and took the new "early retirement payoffs".

For twenty-some years Diana was there, six or seven days a week. She heard the employees' comments and grievances .She knew their pulse. She did a lot of counseling at that time. People thought she understood. Some were actually kinder to her eventually. Some of the employees would be condescending toward her, or make wise cracks about the lawsuit and her husband. This hurt. Especially coming from some of her husband's lifelong friends, people that had been at their home and had eaten pizza with them after work for years. Friends she used to eat supper with at work for many years would sit at another table or turn their heads when they walked by, pretending they didn't see her. She knew that they were afraid to be seen talking or associating with her. One of the other nurses became a target as well, because she was her friend. When she would come home in tears sometimes and told her husband about the disloyalty of their co-workers, he would say: "It's OK, they have to keep their job." She cried sometimes driving to work, and would have rather driven anywhere else.

She had never had many friends, and had just opened up a little in the last few years. There were three or four - oh so loyal – friends throughout that entire time that didn't care what management thought about them. They were the kind of friends that anyone could only dream of having. They would talk her through the hardest times, day by day. Without their support, their humor and their incessant encouragement she would have never made it through the six years, she was sure. She would come home and transfer all this good will and energy onto her husband who was totally isolated from everyone, and could only draw strength from it through her.

There were many months when there was no progress in the legal proceedings. The legal process was slow. Her husband would lose hope many times, and she did as well. He always told her later that he would have never fought this, had it not been for her supporting him.

She had no choice. He did not deserve this. It was an injustice. She had to keep him out of depression.

He had over 900 job rejections. It destroyed his confidence and self-value, and drove home the point of his age. The few interviews he was granted were unproductive, jobs in another state and less than one third of his salary. He was 47 years old when he was fired.

They started a Home Greeting Card Business to try to keep going and working with new interests and challenges. Anything to feel productive and keep their spirits up. Health problems were threatening, surgeries, worries about the children and their problems as they grew into adulthood. It was hard for them as well to carry on and survive in their depressed family environment. They took the kids along for short family vacations, but their depression did not allow for much fun. It felt like a cloud hung over their household. It had put a spell on them all. Her husband would sit in a room for hours with the lights off. He was so sad and detached that one couldn't stand by and watch him. If someone touched him, he would start crying. The kids felt guilty being happy, playing the piano or bringing friends home.

Their marriage survived on pure commitment and love and respect for each other, Diana recalls. They would take turns holding each other up.

They had exhausted all their savings, cashed in insurance policies, lost all their security, which just destroyed her husband, the planner. It was a long process. While hundreds of company attorneys frantically prepared a perfect case of cover-up of the company's age discrimination, her husband worked tirelessly for months with his attorney in preparation for the trial. It took everything they had. It took her fighting spirit and determination as never before in her life – to sustain her husband throughout this six-year federal lawsuit. They did not give up until he won and had his job back and the retirement he had earned for 30 years.

It took even more strength for her to retain her job during those years in the hostile and discriminatory environment at the same company - because of the lawsuit. She could write an entire book about this.

No one could believe that they won that lawsuit. People were in awe. The courtroom was filled with company attorneys and company experts and people paid to testify. Some of their friends had testified for the company. They had no choice if they wanted to keep their job. They understood.

A couple of their true friends sat in the courtroom, too – every day throughout the two-week trial – in support of their cause.

Her husband had counted on the "jury of his peers", and he wanted his job back. His attorney said this would never happen. The company would never allow him to go back to work.

After two hours of deliberation, the "jury of his peers" decided that her husband was discriminated against because of his age. The judge ruled that the company must either reinstate him at his job or pay him his salary, the case was left open to insure compliance. They had won.

The day her husband walked into the work cafeteria – all the people that were scared and intimidated and suppressed the day before - the entire crowd - stood up and cheered. Diana realized that they had changed the face of the workforce and workplace forever, and not only at their company. People would speak out now, and fight for their rights. They had fought and won for everyone. No one at that time had yet challenged a Fortune 500 company on an age discrimination issue and many people had been unjustly fired for no other reason than their age. They also lost their livelihood, their esteem and their retirement.

Her husband was not gloating; he wasn't looking for applause. He never wanted to be a hero. He wasn't after money, all he wanted was to work and earn his retirement. He was respectful throughout this entire ordeal, and he returned to work without animosity. He earned even more of Diana's respect by that, and everyone else's. No one ever was happier going to work every day for the next four years until he was ready to retire.

Their attorney became famous; he was from then on lecturing and consulting on age discrimination cases across our nation, and in Japan. He was quite an authority on this issue, and he deserves their eternal gratitude. He fought with them, and gave everything – just like they did. Her husband's case entered the law books as the standard for jury instructions in that state. It was a precedent setting case.

They sold their apartment building for a profit, and made plans for their future. There was a tomorrow. They bought property in Nevada. They would escape there once in a while – not that they could afford it, but it helped to keep their sanity.

Diana and her husband continued to to her working at this company without incident, but in a stressful environment for four years until they decided that they could afford to retire.

They built a house in Nevada where they loved the climate, the newness, the growth and the excitement. Diana carried the pictures of their house with her literally every day for the last four years of her job. She needed a constant reminder that there was a tomorrow. The six years of the struggle of the lawsuit almost destroyed them. It took much focus and planning, and support from the children and a couple of friends, and a few mini-vacations, to keep them going despite all odds, setbacks and challenges.

There were little lights going on… grandchildren were coming one by one… joys crept back into their lives… their hopes became reality.

They looked back with pride, much like a mountain climber when he finally achieved the plateau he had set his eye on, the goal he had set for himself. There definitely was a tomorrow.

Diana could hear her mother caution: "Beware of this good life."

The first year they lived in their beautiful home in Nevada, she walked around the house at night when all was quiet – in awe - wondering if she wasn't dreaming. The abundance scared her. It seemed like "too much of a good thing". So many huge windows! For a long time she felt that the timer was still running, and she could not believe that she had no more schedules or deadlines to keep.

Or was she afraid that the clock would suddenly stop? She had trouble believing that she deserved all this. Her parents used to say: "When you stand up high, be careful not to fall." You can never be too sure. All her life she was afraid to seize a happy moment, and call it hers, enjoy it, relish it - for fear that she might "jinx" it, and it would crash…

Her husband assured her that he'd be there. He was the rock in her life. She doesn't dream of boots anymore. All her nightmares vanished at last. She never had it so good. They have all the comfort, love and devotion and respect for each other that she never believed she deserved. They can read each other's thoughts, and he was ever protective and supportive. Some people find it hard to get along when they retire and spend so much time together. To her it was very comforting. She choose to reserve space for herself ever so often.

Diana would never again allow herself to totally relax in a sense of security based on anything or anyone other than her own two feet. She needed to stand on her own, needed her own identity, her own place in her very soul – having been uprooted so many times in her life .She still was a rebel.

Diana had to be sixty years old to put her finger on the common and dominating threads that weave throughout the fabric of her life: the lack of freedom and the fear of authority. There was her free spirit, this fine thread that bursts out now and then, fighting for survival.

Diana was brought up in a culture of no choice, a culture that did not allow one to deviate from the traditional, from the norm. This dampened and stifled every sense of individuality, creativity, self-confidence and expression of freedom. As a little child she learned to respect adults "because they were adults." The atmosphere in Germany during the war and Hitler times, her early childhood, was to do or die. One feared authority, if one wanted to stay alive. People lived in a state of subjection, of servitude and degradation, under burdening toil and labor and control like that of slavery. It was a culture of fear and suppression, and absolute loyalty especially for the poor. There was a "code of honor" above all, and ritualistic and spiritual influences in her life that achieved the same result as the religion that taught women to be inferior. She came out of an era of "no freedom of speech" or other freedom. This total respect and fear for authority turned out to be a devastating and destructive force in her life, it dominated her life.

Even writing this – She had to overcome apprehension and fear that no one was going to strike her down as she found the words.

Looking back Diana realized how much she lacked the judgement and control and the freedom of choice. She wished she could have followed her own inner sense and listened to the voice of her soul in determining the direction and purpose of her life without so many intimidating influences. She always did what she was supposed to do. She followed instructions out of necessity and fear. She was not just ignorant and naïve, she loved and trusted and respected what she was taught to believe in. Her beliefs were enslaved and overshadowed by intimidation, by the fear of God and the devil – all the same. Her beliefs were influenced and subdued by the power of the SS and the War, the authority certainly of her parents, priests, teachers, nuns, husband, bosses, as well as institutions, such as: marriage, church, convent, law, and even policemen to this day. It's as if the war machine kept running - not only in a physical, but psychological, emotional, and cultural sense as well.

She was never given the choice to freely follow her heart.

Intimidation was a paralyzing force in her life. It overpowered; it took away her freedom of choice. Diana knew that her beliefs without it would be different. Intimidation violated her basic right to be, to exist. This faceless power – it killed her spirit, it stole her soul. This was the crime of it all.

If she could live her life over – she would humbly ask her creator for one gift, the freedom of choice. She would want to be her own artist, determine the heights her free spirit could fly, carve out her own wants and desires and troubles and conduct her own symphony without someone else setting the stage. She would want to paint her own mural on the canvas of her life – without someone else picking the colors, or pushing the brush.

X

THE   BRIDGE

Diana's life's voyage was not a gentle one. She was put out to sea without knowing how to swim. She broke out of such a different world, and crossed the ocean to a new life, a new country of freedom. It was not "smooth sailing" that made her strong, but weathering many storms and overcoming adversity. There were many storms, and many times she thought she'd drown. Yet here she was, on the other side.

She had built an emotional bridge across the valleys and peaks of her life: times of war, and times of peace. She was now walking back, not with regrets and bitterness, but above it all, looking ahead with faith and forgiveness and empathy, looking for balance between pride and regret, between liberty and honor. She had found resolve, and a place of calm in the very center of her soul –finally after a life of turmoil. It felt like "sitting in a cherry tree", looking down on her life floating by without being threatened by it.

She has knelt down there in the trenches and was rained on plenty. She knew fear and despair and found her way out of many dark tunnels. She looked up to false heroes, took many wrong turns, had rocks falling on her head, but eventually climbed out of it stronger, every time. Someone always saved her at the last minute and the rocks turned out to be blessings... and the sound of boots faded.

Her spirit was mended at last. She walked across the bridge of her life - as a reminder of a turbulent but rich journey, with a humble and compassionate heart for anyone in the valley of his life, and with immense gratitude.

She was thankful for the "times of her life" that molded and branded and tested and tried and formed her character, and made it strong. They made her what she was – a person, she'd dare to say, she was proud of.

Was there passion in her life?

Sometimes Diana wished she could have done things easier, slower, less intensely. However there always was this passionate conviction to a cause - so often not of her own choosing. Regardless, it committed her, drove her, not necessarily with loyalty to herself or for ultimate pleasure at the time, but with the yearning for more, the intense desire for totality in whatever she did or wanted. There always was love of magnificence and wonder, spirituality and a search for inner balance and peace. So much her father!

Whatever she may have lacked in intention or conviction, she made up for in her passion: to make more out of it, to rework it, to make it fit, to finish it, to make it the best. After all, she was her mother's daughter… There was no choice but to be the best she could be, even if she sometimes failed miserably.

It was healthy to open that door to her past, savoring precious memories, as well as reliving hurtful and humiliating experiences – and with resolve at last. Reflecting on her life – as scary as it was – allowed her to embrace her past and her heritage, realizing that she was an extension of the traits and talents, faults and strengths of her ancestors. She was bonded to it, the good and the other, the burdening expectations and the controversies, the dissolutions of ideals and the foundation of honor, integrity and pride. She surely was a survivor. She was a hostage of her heritage. Diana had learned that it was easy to judge and blame, but forgiving was better for the soul - forgiving others with a generous heart, and forgiving one's self for never being enough.

Sometimes Diana felt like she played a role in different life dramas, in very separate settings. She was there, she played the part and she had the scars to prove it. Though it was like someone else pulled the strings…She was thankful for a superior being that surely held her "in the palm of His hand"- and hoping that He will hold her future as well. She had finally learned that "GOD IS LOVE" – regardless of what she was, imperfect and all. At last she had learned to be comfortable with God.

Her faith kept her sane, even though her faith in God had nothing to do with the people that represented Him. She believed in God despite those people, despite all the false heroes in her life.

There was no greater feeling than being at peace with the person you are, and to be in harmony with the universe.

Diana was thankful for her parents' strong character and integrity. They gave her wings strong enough to fly, even against the wind. She could honestly say that she was proud of her heritage now. Now she was thankful for her children with good values and ethics, and hopes for a bright tomorrow. As their mother, she dared them to be "true to themselves." She was thankful for her husband and the life they shared. If they had ten lifetimes together, it would not have been enough. She indulged in spoiling her grandchildren, and building houses for every one of her children just like her parents did.

It didn't feel "selfish" anymore to think: "This is my day, this is my life – I deserve to live it." At last she didn't feel guilty anymore to have it so good. She could laugh and cry when she pleased, and she valued the great blue Nevada sky, sunshine most every day, and not much of winter. She valued a friend, and a hand shake. She valued commitment and love and contentment. She sometimes couldn't believe that she deserved this abundance of happiness and love.

Most of all Diana enjoyed the greatest luxury of all: the freedom to make deliberate choices at last now in her retirement years, nothing all that grand, just on a small scale. It was a great gift. Even the simple fact that she could sleep late if she wanted to, or watch evening movies she never could when she was working, was a luxury to her. She felt very fortunate that she could choose to eat out at sinful buffets, take spontaneous trips to beautiful places and visit her family in Germany sometimes. She could choose lush roses and bougainvillea and palm trees over many other beautiful gardens if that's what she wanted. She could choose the music she liked, the climate that suited her the best, the house with the biggest windows, a swimming pool and a waterfall in her backyard. She could have pretty towels in every color. She was still grateful for milk and bread and potatoes. She could choose to have mirrors all around her now (which she would recommend highly for every child no matter what age). She worked so hard to believe that she was good enough. It took too long a time for her to build up enough confidence to look the world in the face. Now and then she dared to explore her artistic talents, and her custom stained-glass windows reflected her personality, her heritage, and her joy.

Now Diana was looking for alternatives and choices in everything she did. Some choices were encumbered with compromises, but for her it was the greatest feeling to know that she had choices, that she was not forced to accept everything, that she could change almost anything if she wanted it bad enough. It was great to know that there was always another way, and that she was allowed to choose to leave or stay. It was a relief for her to think that she could make wrong choices right, and that if her dreams should ever change, she would be free to re-define them. She wished she had known long ago that she could leave things behind without guilt, that life was but a journey of learning, and that there were no mistakes… She wished she could have been free to change her mind or to take a different path in this big world with a thousand choices.

Diana's favorite time always was the dawn. She cherished the sun coming up every morning – and being alive. She was so grateful for the many tomorrows in her life she hadn't dare hoped for.

XI

REFLECTIONS

Visiting Germany Diana felt like she was transported into a different time. She wondered if any German could understand. She didn't come with a tourist's eye. She saw the shadows of the past.

Behind the hustle and bustle of new generations pushing their way through the narrow streets of Munich Diana felt the ache of the ruins that stood in place of the new buildings. These towering new structures seemed to reach all too desperately for the sky – as if trying to escape the war for every inch of space with the crowded, narrow streets between them. Certainly they were a testament of the industriousness and pride of the German people – their relentless drive to rebuild and their indestructible spirit.

Diana thought to herself that she must have inherited that spirit to rebuild her own several homes and several "lives".

She walked through lush, flowering greens and all colors of bloom in the new parks of Munich. She saw people walking their dogs – or their memories? She saw old people with canes - crippled by the burdens of their past. She saw people in wheelchairs – hoping that the sun might warm up their hearts and stiff limbs. She looked up at the trees - grown so tall you wouldn't think they had any memories. She saw young mothers walking their baby strollers just like forever…

little children screeching for joy as they rolled down the green hills of the lovely park – built on the old garbage dumps of the war.

Diana wanted to call it "Rebirth".

Most churches of Munich and throughout Bavaria - too many to count – were still in the process of repair, still patching the wounds and the brittle walls of the wars of past centuries. Without a doubt they would be rebuilt. They are the heart of generations, their refuge, symbols of age-old faith in a living God. The walls of these churches, adorned with every Saint and every image of hope – still showed despair no less than signs of destruction. If despair could be measured
– these walls would scream! One would think they did. These old confessionals had heard the sins of centuries, and had given absolution to wars. These grand old churches breathed with undeniable power a reverence in the light of history, a presence of a higher authority, worthy of all the magnificent art and splendor. You could hear the "Credo" of children, the cries of the old and the silence of the dead. You could still feel the pulse of the people within these dark walls, and the soul of the past reaching out as to never let one forget where one came from.

The age old pipe organs still played the age old songs to the same age old God. One would think one could hear voices of thousands of generations singing along.

The historical landmark, the Glockenspiel at the town square of Munich – with its dancing figures to the music of the ancient bells - won't ever let the new generations forget the victory over the plague in the year 1348 that took too many lives of their ancestors.

And the train rolled on…alongside her river, her friend after all. It was still.

Diana shuddered as it passed the convent, somewhat obscure in the distance, much too close, all these years later. The train knew no mercy.

Her next stop was Passau, the "big city" of her childhood. It was an ancient Bavarian town and a favorite destination for trade as well as tourists of all ages. Spread out clear to the Austrian border now, it meandered over hills and valleys, over bridges and through tunnels, around the banks of the three rivers (Danube, Ilz and Inn) that unite in the center of the town. You could distinctly see the "colors" of their waters merge – much like the remnants of cultures reaching back to Celtic and Roman times…

It always was her favorite town.

The beautiful castles and fortresses on every hill around were now transformed into "Cafe's", museums and points of interests – as historical treasures. There was a new coat of finish on everything. Yet the charm and idyll of ferns and ivies overgrowing the holes and ruins of the wars reaching back to times of Emperors and Kings and Lordships – were not deceiving her heart. The times of Prince Bishops as Lords of the land told of the strong influence and control of the church. There are the churches such as St. Serenius (a Martyr), dating back to the fifth century AD, or the St. Stephen's Cathedral built in the ninth century housing the world's largest church organ, and so many more.

These churches, the many monasteries, abbeys, defiant citadels spoke of more than met the eye. They spoke of martyrs that died for their convictions and beliefs. They spoke of uprisings and rebellions and bloody battles. They explained the citizenry's sub ordinance and suppression. They explain their devotion to their religion as a way of hoping to break out of their bondage, when all

213

it was doing was keeping them there. The "class-conscious society", as one likes to call European people, stemmed back to historical times with powerful influences of Kings, Barons, Bishops, Lordships – and therefore servants. This atmosphere seemed to hold people there; they always were grounded there.

Diana could see where it was hard to believe in a bright and shining future for young generations. It was hard to understand the "freedom" of such a different world as hers.

Germany today was a free country. How free? It was still burdened and entwined in the turmoil and leftovers of the ongoing wars of the European countries all around it, if not of its own. A small country itself, it was forever supporting fugitives from all over, draining its economy. It was forever trying to recover and rebuild between wars, a legacy throughout the course of history for so many centuries that Diana wondered if when everything was ever all rebuilt, the minds could still recognize freedom?

Would the children ever know what it would be like to really be free?

What was freedom? Was anyone really free? Perhaps it was true that only after living in bondage one can appreciate freedom.

Walking was still dangerous on the crowded, narrow streets of Passau. There were no sidewalks. These streets, weaving through the old town in an unparalleled fashion much like a maze, around sharp bends and narrow tunnels, were testaments of the times without cars. Pray tell what the mosaics of these ancient cobblestone streets would say – could they speak! How many feet have walked over the old planks of stone thresholds into the dark, ancient buildings since the fifth to first centuries BC that made them so rounded and weathered – as smooth as stones in a river? Stones in a river... had time polished all the rough edges – smoothed over the troubled minds, worn off all the rebellious attempts of resistance toward the destined course of history?

Did history "belong" to the past? Diana saw the future entwined in it – hearts and souls, its arms reaching out over generations. It held people close, molding them still, shaping their destinies and keeping them there.

Diana looked in the new windows that somehow didn't fit into the ageless stone storefronts and ruins, now garnished with modern fashions and wares. She wondered...She was compelled to look beyond the newness, the facade, and she saw fervent attempts of people striving for a better future while they were chained to the past...she kept seeing flour sacks, she saw pewter pots and a spinning wheel, she saw a shoemaker barely making a living... a mother nursing a child a thousand years ago, the same as one would today. Would this child be free?

Diana stood at the promenade of the Danube River that left the marks of its water level on its banks for centuries to remember – leaving the old stone houses built at its very edge in the wake of its rage and torrents and its hundreds of floods. This river was a symbol of strength for her at some vulnerable periods of her life. She could safely drown her angst, her tears in it and entrust her secret feelings to be buried, that she could not even admit to herself. It was time to say goodbye to her friend, thankful for keeping her steady when she was about to sink.

Times of yesterday.

It was not possible to ignore the countless reminders of hard times past... Was it not possible to reconcile the present with the past?

Was she disloyal and ungrateful to want to put them behind her? As much as she stood in reverence before the wealth and greatness of her European history – as much as she bowed her head in respect and admiration of her heritage –Diana walked away with a feeling that weighed her down rather than lifting her up.

Times of yesterday…

She wanted to forget the painful reality of the way of life in her parent's time – long in the past - but still living on, this reality that people then accepted as unavoidable. She still had trouble comprehending the hopeless poverty of her ancestors, the fruitless labor and endless struggle for the "daily bread". It was too sad for her to bear. It stared her mercilessly in the face, her, and the children of better times, reminding them that the values and traits of the people of those hard times were the core and backbone of future generations. They live on in all of them after all; they made them who they were. Only that realization gives their parents' slave labor honor and purpose.

Times of yesterday…

Diana wanted to forget the stories of these times as fast as she heard them, even now as an adult – she had locked them away in her mind long ago, and they were too cruel to hear now.

They sat at her sister's kitchen table, Elli and her – she at seventy-three and her at sixty-two – and they cried like little children all the tears they were never allowed to cry. They carried no bitterness in their hearts toward their parents, but an ocean of compassion, forgiving their fury at hopeless and desperate times.

There was no blame.

Diana wanted to…she tried…but she couldn't forget her parent's warnings, "Here is the door! If you disgrace us, don't ever come back." "I'll hack off your hands", their father told them, "if you steal anything". Or when their mother would say, "I'll rip you apart from the middle" - and they would try to imagine this as children. Diana wanted to forget the time when her sister talked back to her mother just once, and her mother said " I should have drowned you at your first bath". Her sister never forgot it and had not yet told anyone this because her lips couldn't utter the words. She also never spoke about her painful memories to anyone in previous visits back home. She really did want to believe that her mother sometimes threatened to run away and leave their father with the "ingrates and misfits". Her sister said she planned in her young mind what she would cook for the family if mother were gone.

Diana realized now what she refused to believe all her life – that when her mother was pregnant with her, and "prayed that God take that child", as she told her once, – she really wished she'd never been born.

Even today they were whispering…feeling guilty to talk about their parents.

Could one blame their parents for being crazed in these times of endless despair?

The unexpected funeral of her last surviving Aunt brought Diana back to the church of her hometown Waldeck for the first time since she had left home at fourteen. She unavoidably found herself reeling in the memories of her childhood, memories she had left behind, memories that had grown somewhat obscure in the distance.

She never wanted to walk this road again.

Diana wished there was another "road to town". This one cut too mercilessly into her conscious mind as it passed landmarks of her past. It was the only road, winding through beautiful forests and pristine country settings, winding around her cherry tree, her childhood home - the house her father built, the cross under the three birch trees that in the end brought the SS to their knees... Did she hear boots in the distance? Did she see her father's belt dangling around the corner?

There was no other road. She had moved far away. She never wanted to walk this road again. Did they have to drive this road? There was no way to avoid the spot where she was raped. Blankets of snow had fallen since then, had covered up one of the most dreadful, shameful secrets of her life. Diana felt an icy chill running down her spine - on this warm summer day as they drove past. She had buried that event. She tried to delete it from her memory. She had denied that it had ever happened. She had almost succeeded.

There were those few drops of blood on her dress...She had tried to wash them out, scrubbing frantically – more to clean her soul than her only dress that she wrapped up very tightly and disposed of in an anonymous trash can...

In the white snow though these red drops of blood stood out like haunting eyes, piercing through her memory... these few drops of blood that the moonlight could not betray that day... nor any day...

She must drive past that spot. There was no other way.

In their church not much had changed in fifty years. The beautiful statue of the "Pieta" still crowned the wall behind the altar – a valuable piece of art from the fourteenth century, a reminder of the plague. The big old cross hanging above – demanding the full focus of the congregation, and rightfully so. At the rear of the church the glass-stained window was still boasting the design by Ingrid Bergmann. The stone reliefs of the twelve "Stations of the Cross" were still mounted on both sides of the walls, reminding her of many a penance for her little sins. The smell of age-old flowers and incense lingered forever; the whitest paint couldn't cover up all the cries and cracks of the deteriorated walls. There was some comfort in the thought that these walls had embraced their town for ages past.

Arriving late after the church was filled, Diana took the very last chair in the back, (She missed the old, majestic pews) as though she intended to make a statement that she no longer belonged, or deserved to be part of this town. As she looked over the blank faces of the crowd that packed the church and the cemetery, she couldn't decide whether they were living or dead, family or strangers – most were relatives after all – or whether she knew or should know anyone anymore. It seemed as though everyone had aged generations.

As she listened to the familiar songs of sorrow and anguish – sinners praying for mercy, carrying too heavy a cross – she cringed. She couldn't breathe. She was certain that not one of the people that filled the church had heard the real message of the Gospel: "Christ has risen!" He promised life after death!

Sitting there in this church she felt like the time had stood still for a thousand years. She realized like never before how much the future was rooted in the past.

Diana hurried to leave before most of the crowd became aware of her presence, which was not possible. Cousins, relatives and "old friends" she never knew she had, descended on her on the steps of the church. They knew her instantly, yet she couldn't remember anyone's name or face. She had to pretend that she knew them, they would be insulted if she didn't. Everyone seemed exuberantly happy to see her, and she made many promises to visit that she couldn't possibly keep.

Why did she want to hide? She didn't feel like the legend, the heroine they made her out to be. She left this town as a child and lived a lifetime away, a lifetime they knew little about, and they couldn't possibly understand who she was today. There was an ocean between them and she belonged to the world on the other side, a world so different from theirs. What did they know about her? They couldn't know her secret apprehensions about being German; they couldn't know how she felt about her relatives and the people of this town. They didn't know how many years she struggled to forget the war, the hunger and slavery, the rape and abandonment, the unkindness and loneliness she felt as a young woman. As hard as she tried, she couldn't remember many pleasant things that would have warranted her loyalty to this town. She felt like she had never belonged.

Everyone was incredibly delighted that she still spoke a fluent German and especially a flawless Bavarian dialect after living in the U.S.A. for so many years, which they interpreted to be loyalty to their country, loyalty to them. Why wouldn't they see her as an outsider, a stranger, the traitor she was? They treated her as though she had never left; they still wanted her to be one of them. Why? Was it because she left?

At the cemetery people Diana didn't even know were greeting and hugging her. "I am your cousin"... "Remember me, we were best friends". Diana felt like all those old crosses and tombstones were hugging her, too. She felt very strange. She appreciated her sisters and brother right at her side. They seemed to enjoy this exuberant welcome she got and showed her off as their pride and joy. It was extremely awkward for her. She felt this sneaky insecurity of being "worthy" of all their attention. Considering her true feelings, it seemed hypocritical at best to allow it, much less stand there and smile.

Diana purposely didn't attend the luncheon afterwards. Somehow it didn't seem proper. Her oldest sister explained that they had to leave, and calmed the gossip of the disappointed town. She would have been the highlight of everyone's day, something uplifting, something new to talk about. One of her cousins told her that funerals are about the only family reunions there. An "old friend" who's name she didn't know was running home without attending the luncheon, because they must stop at her house for coffee and cake. Diana would have had to stop at a hundred places.

Where were all these friends and relatives when she was a lonely child?

Even though everyone was so happy to see her, not one of the people she talked to had a gleam in his eyes when she asked them how they were doing, and not one of them said: "Wonderful, I am fine, I am great, doing well, I am happy". It was rather: "Oh, well, one makes do, one survives", on and on...

Her cousins told her that most people drove long distances to work to cities still, since they could not make a living off the sparse land. However the quality of living had much improved, and no one was starving anymore. Some young people left town. In the last years the interest had focused on tourism, to which the beauty of the countryside lent itself perfectly, tours to the Lusen, and some idyllic spots, ski lifts and much more. There was a Town Hall now, a Post Office and a Bank, a Police Station, some shops and even a Youth Camp, however work was still a problem.

The atmosphere in her hometown still reminded Diana much of long ago. It held people there. Only few broke out of it, and moved to nearby cities. *There still was an air of resolution, acceptance, sadness, and resignation*…Somehow most people didn't see a choice.

Diana had never imagined how much this "home-coming" could challenge her identity. She realized that seeing herself as others saw her was a distorted reflection. She spent her entire life trying to be whoever someone else wanted her to be, trying to please everyone else but herself. She cared more about other's perceptions, opinions and expectations than her own. It was hard to break free of these chains.

At last she could see herself clearly in the light of the freedom she was privileged to enjoy at this time of her life. She cherished the right to be… the right to be who she was.

There in Waldeck, her hometown, her heart stood still at another memorial – their glorious Bavarian Forest – now engulfed in a gray shroud of dead branches bowing in defeat to a "bug" that ate up the arteries of its heart. It seemed like some kind of vengeance of nature. No one knew how to stop it. Diana loved their forest. It was the "Lung" of the land. It survived many wars – and now faced a death of its own. It housed their animals and birds. Their entire town was built from its wood. It saw her grow up. She buried her secrets in its roots and carved her initials in the bark of its trees, she listened to its leaves whisper promises of better…

Her mother left many worries and tears in that forest that grew grass for their cow. She planted young trees for the forestry every year, while she picked its berries and mushrooms and napped in its shade. Her father labored and logged and froze and built the roads through this forest, and it gave their men shelter when they had to hide from the SS. It was their pride, this forest, and their livelihood. In the wake of her forest it was not so hard to leave behind the memories of her childhood and youth that were unkind. She buried her tears and the ghosts of the past with the forest.

As Diana visited her parent's grave, she was saddened. She wished she had known their pain, she wished she could have told them that she understood, she wished she could have made up for the hardship and slavery and humiliation they endured all their life. She told them now – that she loved them. She walked away with a sense of closure; somewhat relieved by the thought that distance was kind.

Was she a coward?

Leaving behind her family – brother and sisters – always left her dealing with a torrent of emotions. Once more her sister sprinkled Holy water over her and her husband, "for "a safe trip", she said. After that visit Diana felt grounded and anchored in a heritage she treasured - the good and the bad. Yet in her soul she was still searching for a way to reconcile the past with the present, the two different worlds of hers, still searching to reconcile turbulence with calm, war with peace. As she crossed the oceans back to the U.S.A. she knew she was going home. She was going home not to the country of her birth, but to the country of her choice…She was going home to her children and grandchildren. She was safe. She was free…

For those who didn't know, I am Diana.

The chains of the past have finally let me go…

Sitting in a cherry tree

It meant the world to me. It wasn't our cherry tree.

We had no tree.

It was a neighbor's cherry tree –Forbidden – yet still today

It is a gentle memory…

It touched the sky, that cherry tree. I felt invisible…untouchable…

Surrounded by its branches hugging me.

It was the only place where I could be. A carefree child…

The closest I could get to being free…

I felt safe high in that cherry tree. It was heaven – where no longer

There were hunger, loneliness and pain.

Something made the fears lose power, and the nightmares fade away

While sitting in the cherry tree….

Manufactured by Amazon.ca
Acheson, AB

30131797R00132